About the author

Chris Alden is a Senior Lecturer in the Department of International Relations at the London School of Economics. He has researched and published on Asian–African relations for over fifteen years. He has previously taught at the University of the Witwatersrand, and held research fellowships at the University of Tokyo, the Ecole Normale Supérieure and the University of Cambridge.

Published by Zed Books and the IAI with the support of the following organizations:

Global Equity Initiative The Global Equity Initiative seeks to advance our understanding and tackle the challenges of globally inequitable development. Located at Harvard University, it has international collaborative research programmes on security, health, capabilities and philanthropy. <www.fas.harvard.edu/~acgei/>

InterAfrica Group The InterAfrica Group is the regional centre for dialogue on issues of development, democracy, conflict resolution and humanitarianism in the Horn of Africa. It was founded in 1988 and is based in Addis Ababa, and has programmes supporting democracy in Ethiopia and partnership with the African Union and IGAD. <www.sas.upenn.edu/African_Studies/ Hornet/menu_Intr_Afr.html>

International African Institute The International African Institute's principal aim is to promote scholarly understanding of Africa, notably its changing societies, cultures and languages. Founded in 1926 and based in London, it supports a range of seminars and publications including the journal *Africa*. <www.iaionthe.net>

Justice Africa Justice Africa initiates and supports African civil society activities in support of peace, justice and democracy in Africa. Founded in 1999, it has a range of activities relating to peace in the Horn of Africa, HIV/AIDS and democracy, and the African Union. <www.justiceafrica.org>

Royal African Society Now more than a hundred years old, the Royal African Society today is Britain's leading organization promoting Africa's cause. Through its journal, *African Affairs*, and by organizing meetings, discussions and other activities, the society strengthens links between Africa and Britain and encourages understanding of Africa and its relations with the rest of the world. <www.royalafricansociety.org>

Social Science Research Council The Social Science Research Council brings much needed expert knowledge to public issues. Founded in 1923 and based in New York, it brings together researchers, practitioners and policy-makers in every continent. <www.ssrc.org>

CHRIS ALDEN

China in Africa

Zed Books
LONDON | NEW YORK

David Philip
CAPE TOWN

in association with

International African Institute
Royal African Society
Social Science Research Council

China in Africa was first published in association with the
International African Institute, the Royal African Society and the Social
Science Research Council in 2007 by

in Southern Africa: David Philip (an imprint of New Africa Books)
99 Garfield Road, Claremont 7700, South Africa

in the rest of the world: Zed Books Ltd, 7 Cynthia Street, London N1
9JF, UK and Room 400, 175 Fifth Avenue, New York, NY 10010, USA

www.zedbooks.co.uk
www.iaionthe.net
www.royalafricansociety.org
www.ssrc.org

Fourth impression 2009

Cover designed by Andrew Corbett
Set in Arnhem and Futura Bold by Ewan Smith, London
index: <ed.emery@thefreeuniversity.net>
Printed and bound in the UK by CLE Print Ltd, Cambridgeshire

Distributed in the USA exclusively by Palgrave Macmillan, a division
of St Martin's Press, LLC, 175 Fifth Avenue, New York, NY 10010.

A catalogue record for this book is available from the British Library
US CIP data are available from the Library of Congress

ISBN 978 1 84277 863 0 hb
ISBN 978 1 84277 864 7 pb

Contents

Acknowledgements

I would like to thank a number of people who were instrumental in either the research contributing to this book or bringing it into being. Robert Molteno, who encouraged me to embark on the book project in the first place, deserves many thanks. Along with Robert, Ellen McKinlay has given generously of her time and insights throughout this project and managed to keep me on track! Rosemary Taylorson, David Birkett, Andrew Harrison and Julian Hosie have shown real enthusiasm in promoting the book, something that is increasingly rare in publishing. And thanks to Ewan Smith for pulling the manuscript together on short notice.

To those who kindly read parts or all of the manuscript I owe a debt of gratitude. Robert, Ellen, Alex de Waal, Ricardo Soares de Oliveira, Dan Large and Wayne MacGregor have provided me with important insights and correctives that have made the book a better piece than it was. Any remaining errors, of course, are attributable to me.

In addition to those listed above, others who have helped me to understand better this relationship between China and Africa, either through discussions or through their work, include Ai Ping, Peter Bosshard, P. J. Botha, Martyn Davies, Carla Freeman, He Wenping, Christopher R. Hughes, Garth le Pere, Li Anshan, Andy Rothman, Barry Sautman, David Shambaugh, Garth Shelton, Shu Zhan, Philip Snow, Riaan Meyer, Ian Taylor, Willem van der Spuy, Michael Yahuda. Sincere apologies to those who I have left out due to haste and memory! The East Asia Project, University of the Witwatersrand, deserves to be 'noted in the minutes' for ushering in this whole research agenda and supporting it unstintingly over the years.

And to Kato, Rachel and Jonathan, who have endured this obsession with China and Africa for a long, long time with patience and good humour.

Abbreviations

AfDB	African Development Bank
ANC	African National Congress
APRM	African Peer Review Mechanism
AU	African Union
CEMEC	China National Machinery and Equipment Import and Export Company
CNOOC	China National Offshore Oil Company
CNPC	Chinese National Petroleum Corporation
DfID	Department for International Development
DRC	Democratic Republic of Congo
ECA	Economic Commission for Africa
FDI	foreign direct investment
FOCAC	Forum on China–Africa Cooperation
FTA	free trade area
GNPOC	Greater Nile Petroleum Operating Company
IGAD	Inter Governmental Authority on Development
IMF	International Monetary Fund
LSE	London School of Economics
MCM	Military Manufacturing Complex
MNC	multinational corporation
MPLA	Movimento Popular de Libertacao de Angola
NEPAD	New Partnership for African Development
NGO	non-governmental organization
OAU	Organization of African Unity
ODA	Overseas Development Assistance
OECD	Organization for Economic Cooperation and Development
ONGC	Oil and Natural Gas Corporation

SOE   State Owned Enterprise

SPLA   Sudan People's Liberation Army

TICAD   Tokyo International Conference on African Development

WTO   World Trade Organization

Introduction

'Rumble rumble of ox carts to haul the priceless cargo.
Heaps, hordes to dazzle the market – men race with the news.
In singing-girl towers to play at dice, a million on one throw;
By flag-flown pavilions calling for wine, ten thousand a cask.
The Mayor? The Governor?
We don't even know their names.
What's it to us who wields power in the palace?'[1]

Lu Yu, 'The Merchant's Joy', late Sung dynasty

On a sunny November morning in Beijing, the streets festooned with enormous 30-foot-high posters of giraffes, elephants and African people in traditional dress, leaders from forty-eight African countries and their entourages made their way through the city and to Tiananmen Square. Among the images of wildest Africa that had wallpapered the city was a feathered tribesman from Papua New Guinea, but if this incongruous detail bothered the African leaders, they did not express it publicly to their hosts. Traffic had been quelled by government decree, reducing the normal conditions of gridlock on the city's broad avenues and myriad of ring roads, which exasperate foreigner and local drivers alike, to an unusually manageable pace. Africa's leaders had brought gifts with them, honouring their Chinese hosts with precious stones and other emblematic cultural artefacts from the continent. The cavalcade of limousines halted outside the Great Hall of the People and African presidents and prime ministers spilled out, walked past the red lanterns swinging from lamp-posts, and mounted the stairs of the conference centre. One by one, under the glare of China's state-run television media, the African leaders entered the Great Hall of the People and slowly walked down the red carpet towards the two diminutive figures in black business suits on the podium. Their hosts, the Chinese premier, Wen Jiabao, and the Chinese president, Hu Jintao, smiled and shook hands with each of their foreign guests for the ubiquitous cameras, and then the African leaders were ushered to seats in the cavernous building that housed the meeting. Over an hour passed before the formal introductions were completed and Hu Jintao could, at last, take the stage and address the ensemble. And with that, the China Africa Summit (or, as it was officially known, the Forum on China–Africa Cooperation, or FOCAC) was opened, signalling the public arrival of a new era in Africa's relations with the outside world.

Over the next two days of the summit, the Chinese media provided non-stop coverage of events, including lengthy feature pieces on African countries and interviews with leaders such as Nigeria's Olusegen Obasanjo and Zimbabwe's Robert Mugabe on national television. During this time, the Chinese government committed itself to an ambitious programme centred on provisions for US$5 billion in loans and credits, the doubling of its development assistance by 2009 and, in a bid that would make China Africa's single largest trading partner, increasing two-way trade to over US$100 billion by 2010. African leaders and business groups met with Chinese counterparts to discuss trade and investment opportunities and by Sunday the watching world was told that US$1.9 billion in new business deals had been signed. Notably missing from the international gathering were African and Chinese NGOs, though some of the former had petitioned the Chinese government to be allowed to attend FOCAC to no avail.

What explains the overnight transformation of Beijing, this brusque city of bureaucrats and party functionaries and capital to 1.3 billion people, into a paean of devotion to Chinese–African friendship? How does one understand the dramatic change in ties between two regions that, with the exception of a brief encounter in the fifteenth century and a flirtation with revolution in the 1960s, remained essentially apart? Why has Africa responded so readily to Chinese entreaties? And what does this event mean for Africa and, indeed, for its erstwhile Western partners, who had only the year before declared their devotion to the continent at a G8 summit in Gleneagles?

To answer these questions one needs to start by looking thousands of miles away from Beijing to the depressions of the 'sudd' in southern Sudan, the swamps of the Niger Delta or even off the wild Atlantic coast of the Bight of Benin where night and day oil rigs pumped the viscous substance called *shiyou*. And inland, to the virgin forests of Liberia, Cameroon, Mozambique and Congo, where local Africans and Chinese worked feverishly at chopping down thousands of hectares of trees for timber to be shipped all the way to some of China's state-owned sawmills in faraway provinces such as Sichuan. And beyond to the copper mines, smelters and iron ore mines in Zambia and Gabon, which had stood idle for a generation but were now working again, this time under the direction of Chinese ownership, or to Ghana, Botswana, South Africa and Nigeria, where China's insatiable demand for minerals had opened up new markets for their products. Led by Chinese petroleum companies flush with massive foreign currency reserves and a strong political mandate, Chinese businesses have been on an acquisition spree for resources across the African continent since 1996.

In exchange for their countries' riches, African politicians have acquired dozens of new parliament buildings, presidential palaces and sports stadiums, all built virtually overnight by Chinese construction companies using Chinese labour numbered in hundreds (sometimes thousands) while unemployed Africans were ignored. New investments and loans may have turned dormant

[margin handwriting: spread of the African continent]

[bottom handwriting: spite restructuring, it was Chinese, t unemployed African labour used.]

Introduction

mines into going propositions again, but Chinese investors had brought with them notoriously low labour standards and a wholesale disregard for the environment that mimicked the pattern of accidental injuries and deaths, periodic strikes and long-standing ecological degradation found back in China. When faced with cheaper Chinese-produced imports, African textile and clothing manufacturers, the backbone of employment for many economies, shed jobs by their tens of thousands. It was for many observers, in short, merely a new twist on an age-old story for Africa, the stripping of its resources by a foreign power to the benefit of a few fabulously wealthy leaders while ordinary Africans were left with a barren heritage. THE ISSUE/CONCERN

But there is another side to this story, one that belies the moral certainties of this simple fable of exploitation. For in addition to new public buildings serving the needs of politicians and bureau-crats in African capitals, these same Chinese construction firms were building dozens of hospitals and schools and, most of all, hundreds of miles of tarmac and railway tracks. In less than a year, in countries such as Sudan, Angola and Ethiopia, which had been accustomed to crumbling transport infrastructure for dec-ades, the Chinese built highways that connected the major urban centres with rural communities. Springing up alongside these physical connections were Chinese mobile telephone networks spreading connectivity throughout the continent, while Chinese communication satellites beamed information to a waiting popu-lation. In the markets of cities, fanning out into the most remote corners of the countryside, the rise of Chinese retail traders and low-cost imported goods meant that many Africans could afford new clothes, shoes, radios and watches for the first time in their lives. Seen from this angle, Chinese involvement, far from being a curse, had actually been the catalyst for development and, with that, a new level of improved livelihoods such as Africa had not known for decades.

... not taking account of local needs and concerns.

4

And, as with all such tales, the truth is cobbled together with myth, making it all the harder to discern (much less assess) the implications of China's role in Africa. 'The Chinese use convict labour' is one persistent rumour that circulated throughout the continent. 'China plans to colonize Africa,' whispers another. Indeed, China's growing public presence in Africa, coming as it does against the backdrop of a sustained Western media campaign of 'shock and awe' at China's new-found power, has set the stage for a misunderstanding that holds disturbing potential for African and global politics generally. It is therefore more important than ever to understand this emerging relationship and its implications for Africa and, with that, the concerns of Western interests.

Partner, competitor or colonizer?

The fast pace of change in Chinese–African relations has provoked much discussion in policy-making, as well as scholarly, circles in Africa, Europe and the United States of late. Underlying much of the existing analysis of Beijing's new role in continental affairs are three contrary strands of thought which can be summarized as China as 'development partner', China as 'economic competitor' and China as 'colonizer'.

- The *first* interpretation ('development partner') holds that China's involvement in Africa is part of a long-term strategic commitment to the continent, one that is driven by its own economic needs, a commitment to transmit its development experience to the continent and a desire to build effective cooperative partnerships across the developing world.
- The *second* interpretation ('economic competitor') holds that China is engaged in a short-term 'resource grab' which, like some Western counterparts, takes little account of local needs and concerns, whether developmental, environmental or with

5

respect to issues like human rights. Coupled with Chinese manufacturing and trade wherewithal, this approach suggests that African development gains are being challenged, if not undermined, by Chinese competitiveness.

- The *third* interpretation ('colonizer') emphasizes that China's new engagement in Africa is part of a long-term strategy aimed at displacing the traditional Western orientation of the continent by forging partnerships with African elites under the rubric of South solidarity. From this perspective, this is a process that will ultimately result in some form of political control over African territories. *Hegemonic challenge?*

The spectacle of international disputes, albeit diplomatic, over events in Sudan is the clearest and most recent expression of the potential for conflicts over oil, human rights and sanctions, and raises the prospects of foreign intervention. As the intemperate commentary on China in Africa grows among political circles in the West – some of it fully deserved, some of it no more than a contemporary version of the fear-mongering 'yellow peril' – an empirically based analysis of the content and context of Chinese involvement in Africa is desperately needed. In particular it would help to clarify the following: (i) the relationship between China's energy policy and its immediate interests in Africa; (ii) the implications of closer trading relations and investment regimes between the two regions; and (iii) the areas of policy friction and policy convergence, and its impact on relations with other external powers, as the Chinese and African governments act to consolidate the relationship. Moreover, as ties between China and Africa grow in depth and complexity, the relationship will increasingly be determined not by government declarations and deal-making between elites but rather through the experiences of individual Chinese and Africans in all walks of life. Developing an informed understanding of the three visions of Chinese

* Key relationships / dynamics

engagement with Africa, ranging from the constructive to the malevolent to the benign, that are shaping the responses of African states, business and civil society, and concurrently the reaction by Western actors, will pave the way for a measured response to this dynamic new relationship.

Book outline

This book will investigate the emerging relationship between China and Africa and seek to assess the character and content of China's foreign policy towards the continent. To assess and determine which vision – partner, competitor or colonizer – is representative of China's approach to the continent, the book will shed light on the role of resources as a driver, the residual position of the ideology, and the influence of the recognition issue on shaping Beijing's priorities in Africa. Moreover, it will give attention to the instruments of implementation, Chinese state-owned international corporations, Chinese foreign aid (Overseas Development Assistance, or ODA), as well as the emergence of Chinese immigrant communities in part of Africa. Concurrently, the book will examine the response of African states and society to China's foreign policy and presence, focusing in particular on the influence of African regime type and political economy as a guide to understanding their reaction to emergent China. Finally it will analyse the impact that Chinese activism in Africa will have for Western concerns, both commercial and normative, on the continent.

To analyze the Chinese intent and behaviour, we need to consider their FOREIGN POLICY (which 1 of the 3 characters does it embody?), energy concerns, ODA projects. FURTHERMORE, the African response.

1 | China's new foreign policy towards Africa

China's growing public presence in Africa has captured the world's imagination. The recent foray of Beijing, once a fervent participant in the cold war in Africa, into the continent has been characterized not by ideological considerations but by a singular focus on resource acquisition and commercial opportunism. Two-way trade, which stood at less than US$10 billion in 2000, had surged to over US$50 billion by the end of 2006, making China the continent's third-largest trading partner after the United States and France. In the same period China's share of Africa's exports jumped from 2.6 to over 9.3 per cent and it has become the leading trading partner for several of the continent's commodity-based economies.[1] Nothing symbolized Africa's importance to the Chinese economy so succinctly as Angola becoming China's largest foreign supplier of oil, passing Saudi Arabia in 2006. Africa has featured prominently on the Chinese diplomatic circuit, benefiting from no fewer than five major tours between 2005 and 2007 by Chinese leaders, as well as a heads-of-state summit in Beijing in November 2006. And while a decade ago there was little evidence of China in Africa, today there are hundreds of major Chinese businesses, bolstered by tens of thousands of Chinese labourers, retailers and even tourists.

At the core of China's rapid entry into African markets is its deliberate promotion of a foreign policy of 'no political strings' which, when coupled with Beijing's willingness to provide aid and concessionary loans, has proved to be tremendously appealing to African leaders. Capital-rich, technologically proven and harbouring a sense of political entitlement, China has embarked on a global search for untapped resources, new markets and reliable diplomatic partners in which Africa features prominently. And while African resources are vital to the health of the Chinese economy, the continent also occupies an important place in China's global ambitions as well. China's emergence as a key player in Africa, the impact of its presence and its challenges to traditional Western pre-eminence in African economies all form critical components of this dynamic new relationship.

This chapter will investigate Chinese foreign policy towards Africa by, first, examining the drivers and instruments of China's contemporary engagement with the continent as well as the wider context within which its Africa policy has developed. Second, the chapter will focus on the key structure and institutions involved in shaping China's Africa policy. Third, it will assess the ideological sources of China's contemporary involvement, including the role of history in constructing a foreign policy that would appeal to both African needs and interests. Finally, it will conclude with a preliminary analysis of the impact of China's foray into Africa among African elites.

The development of China's foreign policy towards Africa

Though the official rhetoric of continuity speaks otherwise, the fact is that from the opening of official ties with Egypt in 1956, China's engagement with Africa has been episodic, shifting from periods of intense activity in the 1960s and early 1970s to outright neglect for much of the 1980s. To understand the changing dynamics in China's approach to Africa, it is necessary to place it in the context of Chinese foreign policy from the inception of the Communist Party government in 1949 to the rediscovery of Africa in the contemporary period.

Since the founding of the People's Republic of China, the leadership has wrestled with the dilemmas posed by a need to restore the country to its historical standing as a leading power against the backdrop of its own considerable development challenges. Caught between its aspirations and the realities of technological backwardness and poverty, the new government sought to carve out a position as the world's leading developing country within the context of the dismantling of European empires under the shadow of its own alliance with the Soviet Union. As relations with the post-Stalin Soviet Union deteriorated, China's claims to Third World leadership – manifested in Mao Zedong's 'Three Worlds' policy – put it at the forefront of ideological and military support for revolutionary regimes and anti-colonial struggles.[2] Notably, this claim to leadership was not exercised through engagement with the standard bevy of Third World organizations such as the Non-Aligned Movement, but 'at an aloof distance'.[3] This period of support for revolutionary change in the Third World was followed by the self-imposed isolation of the Cultural Revolution. Relations with far-flung areas like Africa were severely curtailed as the Chinese political system turned on itself in a struggle for both the leadership of the country and the economic direction that it should ultimately take.

In 1978 the new leader, Deng Xiaoping, set China on a gradualist road of capitalist-oriented development that produced three decades of nearly double-digit growth and a rising in living standards that has brought a ninefold increase in per capita income to US$1,700 in 2005.[4] In the course of this phenomenal economic growth, the number of those suffering poverty in China was reduced from 280 million in 1978 to 140 million in 2004.[5] Bolstering Deng's foreign policy was, with the notable exception of the contentious issue of Taiwan, a benign relationship with the United States and a welcoming approach to foreign direct investment (FDI). The shock of the emergence of a nascent democracy movement and the subsequent crackdown in Tiananmen Square in 1989 instigated a debate within the Communist Party as to the direction the country should take, a situation that was resolved only with Deng's 'Southern Trip' in 1991. Deng's recommitment to transforming the economy was coupled to an admonition on the best approach to foreign policy: 'Observe calmly, secure our position. Hide our capabilities and bide our time. Be good at maintaining a low profile, never claim leadership.'[6] This became the new watchword for Chinese foreign policy, helping the country to weather the international firestorm of criticism in the aftermath of Tiananmen and reasserting its standing as a leading foreign investment haven. China's emerging capitalist economy (or, as the official jargon preferred to call it, 'socialism with Chinese characteristics') moved into higher gear as the reforms were extended to other regions. Running alongside this renewed commitment were considerable developmental challenges arising out of the torrid streak of economic growth, from increasing inequality between the prosperous coastal belt and the interior to the decrepit condition of the loss-making State Owned Enterprise system. In particular, the certainties of self-sufficiency – a central pillar of Chinese policy since 1949 – in a host of areas vital to development such as energy, strategic minerals, forestry resources and even food production no longer could be maintained. Even the famous Daqing oilfields, whose discovery and exploitation had inspired ideological campaigns in the 1960s, were beginning to run low under the combined weight of accelerating Chinese needs, technological shortfalls and general mismanagement. At the same time, China's economic development had begun to produce significant foreign currency reserves and, tied to their growing technical and managerial expertise, the possibility arose that Chinese themselves would be able to address these resource deficiencies. The situation was ripe for outreach to a new source of energy and natural resources – Africa.

Chinese engagement, African resources and new markets For Africa, China's transition from an oil exporter to an oil importer in 1993 was a significant milestone in its development. Chinese officials recognized that, in order to maintain the roaring pace of its economy, the country would need to have secure sources of energy as well as other critical resources.[7] China's current strategy of engaging developing countries and locking in their resources through government-to-government agreements is an outgrowth of this recognition, coupled with their appreciation of the dangers of political instability from Middle Eastern sources. It is for this reason, inspired primarily by the American-led military intervention and occupation of Iraq in 2003 as well as the serious disputes over Iran's nuclear programme, that Africa is in the process of assuming greater prominence in China's global strategic calculus. Already, over 31 per cent of all of China's oil imports are sourced from Africa, and that is set to expand further with the purchase of significant stakes in Nigeria's delta region.[8]

Africa's relatively unexploited energy sources, timber, agriculture and fisheries offer the Chinese a unique opportunity to lock in through formal or informal means a steady supply of key resources. Big projects, such as the investment in Sudan's oil industry from 1996 onwards, whereby the China National Petroleum Corporation has transformed an energy sector plagued by war and Western sanctions into the country's leading export (with China as its top destination, providing nearly 10 per cent of its oil requirements), are clearly at the forefront of China's interests in Africa. With a 40 per cent share of the Sudanese government's Greater Nile Petroleum Corporation, China's leading oil multinational has demonstrated its ability to manage all facets of a petroleum extraction operation to international industry standards. Indeed, industry analysts have pointed out that PetroChina's position in Sudan has served as an important platform for attracting the interests of oil-rich countries in both Africa and the Middle East. Equivalent investments, if not as significant to Chinese domestic consumption, have been made by Chinese multinationals in Nigeria, Angola and Gabon, as well as purchases of shares in Algeria's natural gas fields. Linked to these investments are projects aimed at improving the physical infrastructure of these countries, especially roads and port facilities, which enhance the attractiveness of Chinese ventures to African governments as well as improving the export efficiency of these enterprises. Here Chinese companies have often successfully outbid their Western counterparts (as well as those of other developing countries such as India, Brazil and South Africa) through the traditional strategies of linking investment to tie-in projects and providing lower labour costs in the form of less costly managerial staff and by introducing their own contract workers.

Energy resources are the most important focus of China's involvement on the continent, and occupy the bulk of the thrust of its investment and diplomacy, but other forms of resource-based commercial engagement with Africa play an important part in shaping trade and investment ties, among these commercial logging in Equatorial Guinea and Liberia, cotton and sisal plantation agriculture in Tanzania, the rehabilitation of transport infrastructure in Botswana, new investments in textile manufacturing in Zambia and Kenya and the installation of sophisticated telecommunications systems in Djibouti and Namibia. Some of these ventures are promoted and managed not by high-profile Chinese multinationals but by small and medium enterprises. For example, in China's third-largest trading partner in Africa, Nigeria, non-oil exports topped US$500 million in 2004 based on the sale of agricultural products such as cotton and timber products, both of which involve Chinese companies or joint ventures. Chinese construction firms have played an increasingly prominent role in infrastructure development in all corners of Africa, often gaining a foothold in local markets through close bidding on Chinese government-sponsored projects. The Chinese government has established eleven Trade Promotion Centres around the continent and Chinese businesses are actively encouraged to see Africa as a trade and investment destination. Over 800 Chinese companies are doing business in 49 African countries, with 480 involved in joint ventures with African firms.[9] Thousands of Chinese retail trading shops are now strung across much of the continent, selling low-cost and low-value products made in China directly to Africa's rural population. The product of individual entrepreneurship, these shops are generally family owned and staffed and rely upon a supply chain stretching back to Hong Kong and the mainland. Criminal gangs from Hong Kong have moved into Africa as well, joining other unscrupulous traders who use front companies to illegally export everything from timber, diamonds and products based on endangered wildlife back to China.

The result of all this economic activity is a sharp increase in trade between the two regions. Total trade between China and Africa stood at US$10 billion in 2000, rising to US$18 billion in 2003 and exceeding US$50 billion in 2006.[10] Moreover, Chinese investment in energy resources has played a key role in propelling African growth figures into an annualized rate of over 5 per cent in 2005.[11] While oil is the top item imported from Africa, hardwood timber occupies the second spot, with Liberia, Gabon and Equatorial Guinea serving as leading exporters and though oil-rich Angola has become China's top trading partner in Africa, supplying 18 per cent of its total imports of petroleum, even countries like Ethiopia, with only limited natural resources, have seen their trade with China double from US$150 million in 2003 to US$300 million in 2005.[12] In the course of this dynamic development, China has become the continent's third-largest trading partner after the United States and France and a leading investor, topping US$15 billion in 2004 alone. At the same time, substantial trade deficits with China characterize all but a few countries, such as Angola, Gabon and Zambia, whose escalating resource trade with China offsets the uninterrupted flow of imports of Chinese-manufactured products.

History and solidarity in the forging of China's Africa policy

Since the Chinese leader, Jiang Zemin, visited the African continent in 1996 and officially set relations on a non-ideological footing with an emphasis on resource acquisition, the challenge of Chinese foreign policy towards Africa has been to frame this new approach in terms that would appeal to sceptical African governments. In their favour, in contrast to Western countries, was a solid record of support for independence (though one blemished by occasionally backing the 'wrong' liberation movement, as in Angola and South Africa). Moreover, though acknowledged as small in overall quantity, China's construction of the TanZam railway and the role of barefoot doctors and agricultural specialists in West Africa were remembered positively in Africa. The last challenge facing the Chinese government was to communicate the fact of China's rise as a major economic power and the accompanying capacity of its emergent multinational corporations to compete successfully with long-established Western partners.

Four quotations capture the Chinese government's attempt to construct a relationship with African states, which is founded on a mutual development agenda, shared values and, in the global context, a common analysis of threat. Drawing from public statements on China–Africa relations made by Chinese officials over the past decade, the Policy White Paper declares: 'Sincerity, equality and mutual benefit; solidarity and common development: these are the principles guiding China–Africa exchange and co-operation.'[13] Coupled with this is Premier Wen Jiabao's declaration that 'We do offer our assistance [to Africa] with the deepest sincerity and without any political conditions.'[14]

The emphasis on self-interest mingled with shared experiences and developmental aims is seen to be the 'common project' that encapsulates the rationale for a renewed engagement between China and Africa. A leading Chinese scholar on African affairs, He Wenping, adds, 'Common sense about human rights and sovereignty is only one of the common values shared by China and Africa.'[15] This suggests that the Chinese government sees an abiding cultural as well as political context, born of a common historical experience of the international system felt both by Chinese and Africans, for interpreting the relationship between individuals and the state.

And finally Wen Jiabao, the Chinese premier, stated at the China Africa Cooperation Forum in Addis Ababa in 2003 that the broader global strategic purpose of forging closer ties with Africa was to counter Western dominance. He said pointedly, 'Hegemony is raising its ugly head.' This position certainly resonates with many African elites, for whom the unadulterated use of conditionalities by Western donors has been seen as a threat to their own position.

These fundamental principles form the basis of the new terms of engagement as expressed by China. As presented, however, they still did not address what is an unprecedented and concerted surge of investment, political ties and migration by Chinese interests into Africa. For this, the authorities in Beijing turned to the historical past for inspiration.

Remembrance of things past As Beijing is adamant in pointing out, China's contemporary engagement with Africa is not 'new' but in fact has its roots in policies pursued since the mid-1950s as well as earlier historical precedents.[16] Africa in the cold war era was seen primarily by Chinese leaders as a terrain for ideological competition with the Soviet Union and the United States, as well as the remaining European influences. This took the form of Chinese diplomatic and military support in southern Africa, for example, for liberation movements that were ideologically committed to Maoist China as opposed to the Soviet Union. Moreover, Chinese officials recognized that, with their numerical advantage in the General Assembly and anti-colonial perspective, independent African states held the key to removing the Republic of China from its official status as occupant of the coveted permanent seat on the UN Security Council.

While the onset of the Cultural Revolution in the late 1960s put paid to overt Chinese political activism on the continent, Chinese Overseas Development Assistance (ODA) continued to be a feature of relations. The most notable expression of this was the construction of the TanZam railway between 1970 and 1975, linking Zambia to the coastal port of Dar es Salaam and thus breaking the dependency on white-ruled Rhodesia. Apparently the decision to build the railway grew out of a direct request from Zambian president Kenneth Kaunda, seconded by his Tanzanian counterpart, Julius Nyerere (who greatly admired Mao's collectivization strategies and applied these ideas as part of the Ujaama villagization scheme), to Mao. Interestingly, many of the aspects of Beijing's current approach to African relations reflect the impulses and decisions of that era. These include the government's responsiveness to elite declarations African priorities, the use of state resources and preference for Chinese labour to construct infrastructure projects, and the signature of a high-profile prestige project to mark relations.

Finally, the saliency of the past for contemporary China–Africa relations is reflected in the degree to which Chinese officials feel compelled to summon it in their dealings with African states. In Sudan, for example, Beijing peppers its bilateral diplomatic events and official communiqués with references to General Charles 'Chinese' Gordon, who helped suppress the Taiping rebellion in the 1860s, and upon being transferred to the Sudan,

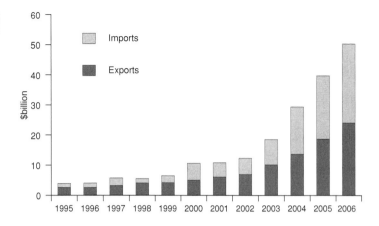

Figure 1.1 China's Africa trade, 1995–2006[17]

was put under siege and killed by the forces of the Mahdi in 1885. The Chinese claim that this event, which 'finally punished' the imperialist, brings the two states closer together. Equally, the Chinese government likes to underscore how African slaves, who escaped from their Dutch masters on the then colony of Formosa, 'fought shoulder to shoulder' with the Chinese general Zheng Chenggong's forces in 1664.[18] Here the implications that China and Africa can cooperate to fight similar 'rogue' forces on Formosa (the island being, of course, the host to the Taiwanese government) to restore Chinese sovereign rule are clearly drawn. The forging of Chinese relations with the coastal states in eastern and southern African is characterized as merely the revival of ties instigated in the late fifteenth century by the Ming dynasty's Admiral Zheng He. Crucially, as Chinese officials are quick to highlight, the presence of what was the world's largest fleet with sixty-three junks and 28,000 men did not result in conquest or humiliation of Africans but rather a brief trading and diplomatic venture.[19] The analogy with the contemporary relationship is, of course, never far from the surface, as the Chinese ambassador to South Africa reminded Africans in 2007:

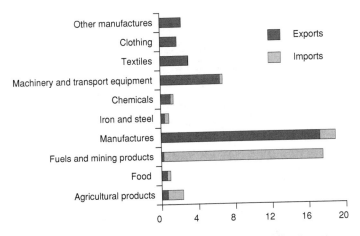

Figure 1.2 China's Africa trade by sector, 2005 ($billion)[20]

Zheng took to the places he visited [in Africa] tea, chinaware, silk and technology. He did not occupy an inch of foreign land, nor did he take a single slave. What he brought to the outside world was peace and civilisation. This fully reflects the good faith of the ancient Chinese people in strengthening exchanges with relevant countries and their people. This peace-loving culture has taken deep root in the minds and hearts of Chinese people of all generations.[21]

At this point in time, the employment of history still dominates the shaping of African elite responses to China. Those elements within the West promoting a 'discourse of fear', which is manifested in its analysis of China–Africa relations, are largely absent from African sources (though this does not, as noted above, mean that there is an absence of criticism of China within Africa, as will be shown in Chapter 3).[22] In this regard, the West should not underestimate the near-universal displeasure, exhaustion and disappointment (if not outright hostility) that Africans feel towards it. A good measure of this can be seen, much to the dismay of his critics, in the consistently positive responses that

19

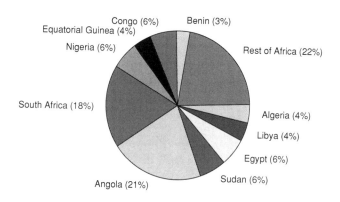

Figure 1.3 China's top ten trade partners in Africa, 2006[23]

Mugabe receives from fellow elites and the population as a whole (though not among fellow Zimbabweans) whenever he travels in other parts of the African continent.[24] The West's employment of conditionalities, merely the latest in the decades of humiliating experiences at the hands of former colonial powers and the United States, echoes the humiliations of the 'unequal treaties' foisted on China by the West in the nineteenth century. Indeed, China's ability to recognize this is part of the genius of its foreign policy endeavours towards Africa. While this invocation of the past in the service of current interests is certainly no substitute for concrete actions, and increasingly Chinese foreign policy is being judged on Africans' contemporary experiences of China, there is no doubt that it has enabled China to achieve an unparalleled prominence in Africa in an extraordinarily short period of time.

Diplomacy and development assistance

A key dimension of Chinese engagement with Africa is its diplomatic crusade aimed at displacing Taiwan's official relations with African countries. The battle for diplomatic recognition between Beijing and Taipei has, of course, been a cornerstone of Chinese foreign policy since the declaration of the People's Republic of China in 1949 and has guided China's Africa policy since Zhou Enlai's Africa tour of 1963–64 when he famously declared Africa to be 'ripe for revolution'. African states were instrumental to Beijing's strategy of voting the Republic of China (as Taiwan was referred to) out of the permanent seat in the UN Security Council in 1971. Despite this major setback, Taipei's diplomacy has proved reasonably successful in retaining official support in many parts of Africa until 1997, when post-apartheid South Africa jettisoned its diplomatic links with the island. The so-called 'dollar diplomacy' used by Taipei, which involved financial support for friendly governments as well as modest aid and investment programmes, was increasingly dwarfed by Beijing's willingness to use its resources to gain diplomatic ground.[25] Moreover, the diplomatic practices of the past, which saw China summarily 'punishing' those states which broke diplomatic ties with it by withdrawing foreign assistance and other projects, have been replaced with a more flexible approach that allows for selective involvement of businesses and Chinese provincial representatives, emphasizing the mix of pragmatism and necessity that characterizes China's new Africa policy.

In October 2005 the loss of Senegal, a key state in the francophone constellation of leading African nations, to Beijing put the rebel island province in the unenviable position of holding diplomatic relations with some of Africa's most impoverished countries, unstable kingdoms and corrupt petro-states.[26] This was followed in August 2006 by the Chadian government's decision to cut official ties with Taipei in favour of Beijing, bringing the total number of states recognizing Taiwan down to five. This final push from Beijing to win over recalcitrant African states in advance of the China Africa Summit meeting in 2006 was seen to be a fitting culmination of its forty-year policy of isolating Taipei on the continent.

Africa's importance to Chinese diplomacy is further under-scored by its numerical advantages as the largest single regional grouping of states and its tendency towards 'bloc voting' in multi-lateral settings such as the United Nations and its agencies. With an outlook that, despite the recent emphasis on 'good govern-ance' emanating out of the West and some African circles, is solidly statist in orientation, African governments have proved to be a reliable source of support whenever Chinese conduct has been criticized. For instance, African votes have been crucial for China in areas as different as the International Olympic Commit-tee decision to award the 2008 Olympics to Beijing and block-ing resolutions tabled at the UN Commission on Human Rights which condemn Chinese human rights abuses. In the words of Premier Wen Jiabao: 'China is ready to co-ordinate its positions with African countries in the process of international economic rules formulation and multilateral trade negotiations.'[27] Beijing officials are said to believe that this strategic relationship with Africa will give it, at relatively low cost, the means to secure its position in the WTO and other multilateral venues.

A crucial component of expanding China's presence in Africa has been the use of foreign assistance to cement ties with gov-ernments as a means of securing resources and winning new diplomatic allies. Africa commands the largest percentage of China's development assistance (44 per cent, or US$1.8 billion), with ODA divided between tied aid, outright grants to recipients, a limited number of loans and new mechanisms such as govern-ment guarantees for sectoral investment in the region. China has been a consistent aid partner of Africa, providing it with a total of US$4.9 billion in foreign assistance between 1957 and 1989.[28] The conflation of 'cooperation' and 'aid', however, coupled to the opaque character of China's foreign assistance (China does not publish details annually, as do countries in the OECD), means that much has to be inferred from public announcements. Most of the aid that it does supply is bilateral and tied to the use of Chinese firms and supplies, though a smaller percentage of Chinese aid towards Africa is filtered through multilateral channels such as the World Health Organization and other UN agencies.

Since Zhao Ziyang's trip to Africa in 1982, the emphasis on cooperation and aid that holds economic gains for China has become official policy.[29] Gifts in kind, the construction of specific facilities such as a sugar mill, and the sending of technical teams to manage these sites are all standard features of Chinese foreign assistance. The use of Chinese firms and Chinese-sourced materials, which has become a matter of some controversy recently, has in fact been a consistent component of China's aid programme.[30] Prestige projects, such as public buildings and stadiums, have also played an important part in securing agreements with African governments. Examples of this include the construction of an extension to the building housing parliament in Uganda, new offices for the ministries of foreign affairs in Angola and Mozambique, presidential palaces in Harare and Kinshasa, and stadiums in Sierra Leone and the Central African Republic. This form of symbolic diplomacy has great appeal to African elites who welcome the opportunity to replace colonial-era public buildings, as well as being a vivid demonstration of Chinese largesse. Moreover, the shift towards profit-making in the early 1980s has meant that Chinese engineering firms have used government-financed construction projects to gain a foothold in the local African market, setting up offices and bidding for contracts.

The key institutions involved in foreign assistance and cooperation are the Ministry of Commerce (formerly known as the Ministry of Foreign Trade and Economic Cooperation), the Ministry of Foreign Affairs and the state-owned banks, such as China Export-Import Bank. The overall budget for foreign aid is prepared by the Ministry of Finance, but it is the Ministry of

Commerce's Department of Foreign Aid which is responsible for planning and management of funds and their disbursement. Monitoring and evaluations also feature in the work of the ministry.[31] An Economic Councillor based in the Chinese embassy abroad is responsible for administration and oversight in each individual country. The Ministry of Foreign Affairs is involved in the organization – though not implementation – of humanitarian assistance along with other ministries.

The China Export-Import (Exim) Bank, along with less visible players such as the China Development Bank, occupies a central role in Beijing's contemporary outreach to African governments. Established in 1994, the China Exim Bank is a government-owned institution under the State Council whose principal activities are to support the expansion of Chinese business by providing finance export credit and international loans for overseas construction and investment, and offering official lines of credit.[32] Based on a comparison with equivalent financing institutions in the United States, Japan and Britain that lend in Africa, the Chinese Exim Bank has a larger portfolio, with US$15 billion being extended in support of a host of projects in 2005 – thirty times greater than that of its nearest rival.[33] Interestingly, one assessment of its impact on international lending in Africa finds that it deviates from established OECD 'best practice' in its willingness to ignore potential environmental impact and social standards for given projects. Indeed, the political imprint on China Exim Bank lending is evident in that weak reporting requirements are imposed on the Chinese firms and there is an apparent willingness for them (as government-owned or managed firms) to operate at a loss.[34] This effectively both compels and subsidizes, for example, Chinese construction companies that take up the infrastructure projects that dominate the bank's portfolio and operate at margins that, without the state role, would not be viable under a strictly commercial reading (see

Chapter 2).[35] It has sought to develop a working relationship with continental and regional banks, such as the African Development Bank (AfDB) and the East African Development Bank. In the case of the AfDB, the China Exim Bank and the China Development Bank have looked into co-financing and parallel financing of projects as one outgrowth of China's hosting of the AfDB annual meeting in Shanghai in May 2007. Finally, in contrast to multilateral and bilateral Western lending agencies, the Chinese Exim Bank's lending is more flexible, less risk adverse and responsive to African governing-elite needs.

Military cooperation and the growth of arms sales are an important aspect of relations with some African governments, especially those under threat owing to civil war, insurgency or even domestic opposition but which are barred from obtaining weapons from traditional Western sources. China's arms sales to Africa stood at US$1.3 billion in 2003, more than double those of Britain but considerably lower than those of Russia whose US$7.6 billion worth of weapons make it the leading arms exporter to the continent. While China supplies only 6–7 per cent of all arms delivered to Africa,[36] Chinese weaponry has nevertheless proved to be significant in some of Africa's bloodiest conflicts, especially in the Horn of Africa, where decades of civil war in Sudan and Ethiopia have provided a welcome market for foreign arms merchants. In particular, Chinese weapons manufacturers have actively targeted pariah regimes like Sudan and Zimbabwe (which have been barred from purchasing from Western sources), providing them with armaments and heavier equipment, including helicopters and Shenyang fighter jets. In a demonstration of versatility, Chinese companies like Norinco (which supplies a range of military equipment to Ethiopia) are also involved in civil engineering projects such as road and dam building in their client country.[37] During the late 1990s, light arms and ammunition from China have been shipped through Dar es Salaam and on to the conflict in the Democratic Republic of Congo, while Chinese arms played an important role in Sierra Leone's civil war, in the Ethiopian–Eritrean conflict and more recently in the conflicts in Darfur and Chad. The Chinese have set up three small arms factories in Sudan that produce light weapons for use in the region, as well as in Uganda.[38] And the Nigerian government's frustration with US congressional interference in the delivery of patrol boats for the troubled delta region contributed to its decision to switch to Chinese military equipment. In this case, the Nigerian purchase of twelve Shenyang fighter jets and missiles, along with a Chinese commitment to train Nigerian technicians in satellite operations, happened in concert with its awarding of oil contracts to China in 2005 and 2006.

Though this has been less publicized in the Western press, China has broken its own past precedents and actively participated in UN-sanctioned peacekeeping operations in part of Africa. Chinese peacekeeping has expanded across the continent, starting with a large contingent in Liberia (a country where Taiwan briefly achieved diplomatic recognition) and smaller attachments to UN missions in the Democratic Republic of Congo and even the Sudan.[39] All in all, over three thousand Chinese peacekeeping troops have participated in seven UN missions on the continent.[40] The majority of Chinese peacekeepers, in fact, are based in Africa, making China the largest contributor of all the permanent member states of the UN Security Council to peacekeeping operations. Concurrently, it has also provided financial support to combat drought in the Horn of Africa amounting to a modest US$200,000 in 1999 and US$610,000 in humanitarian assistance in 2004 to address the Darfur crisis. In a dramatic step aimed at countering critics of its role in Sudan, the Chinese government announced in the middle of 2006 that it would be providing US$3.5 million in support of African Union peacekeeping operations in that strife-torn region.

More recently, Beijing has expanded its foreign assistance programme in Africa to include a Chinese volunteer youth corps, mirroring volunteer youth services like the US Peace Corps and Japan's volunteer corps. Drawn from the Communist Youth League of China, these idealistic youths will use their training in health, agronomy, animal husbandry and linguistics to assist Africans and generally serve as goodwill ambassadors. Three hundred are expected to be placed across Africa by 2009. Again, like the Chinese government's provisions for debt cancellation, humanitarian assistance and even the China–Africa summit process, this initiative suggests that while China's Africa policy has built upon its solidarity ties, it none the less owes much of its contemporary approach to a conscious effort to match the measures undertaken by other leading external powers involved in Africa.

Structures and institutions of Chinese foreign policy towards Africa

One of the complicating factors in understanding China's Africa policy has been the fact that it is being conducted on a fairly rigid bilateral basis, though it is folded into a very public regional diplomacy setting (FOCAC) and sometimes plays out at the multilateral level. This three-dimensional approach has perplexed observers, who have pointed out the gap between the rhetoric of partnership with the ideals and institutions of African regionalism being promoted by Beijing and China's persistent use of bilateral channels to conduct its serious policy initiatives.[41] In fact, this approach has allowed the Chinese to highlight their ties with individual African leaders, something that is well appreciated by individual politicians who might otherwise be neglected on the world stage, while benefiting from the kudos that comes with supporting the pan-Africanist ideals and institutions. Again, like so many Chinese initiatives in Africa, this multi-dimensional approach reflects the prevailing circumstances China finds on the continent and an ability to define and pursue its own interests in light of these circumstances.

In the first instance, bilateral diplomacy is the arena where the resource diplomacy and its ties to China's development assistance and cooperation policies take place. The Taiwan recognition issue features prominently here, though it is consolidated through public declarations at the regional and multilateral levels. Promotion of multinational companies, bilateral trade frameworks and the opening of markets also feature at the government-to-government level, as does the all-important cultivation of presiding African elites by Beijing. The key actors setting the broader foreign policy aims of Chinese foreign policy-making are the Chinese Communist Party leadership, the Politburo and its subcommittees (known as Leading Small Groups).[42] All major initiatives and strategic shifts originate at this national level. As mentioned above, the bureaucratic institutions charged with implementation of foreign policy aims operate under the auspices of the State Council and include the Ministry of Commerce, the Ministry of Foreign Affairs and the China Exim Bank. An increasingly influential institution with respect to China's Africa policy is the State Council's National Development and Reform Commission, whose role in fostering long-term macroeconomic strategies and focus on energy security has given it a greater mandate in shaping the directions of Chinese investments and related initiatives in Africa. Notably, many top officials in China have worked in Africa during their career and have experience in multilateral institutions, unlike their counterparts in the West. These include the former foreign minister, Li Zhaoxing, who served in Kenya and Lesotho, as well as being China's ambassador to the UN.[43]

Complicating this more conventional portrayal of the structures and institutions of China's Africa policy, however, is the relative prominence given to sub-state – that is provincial and municipal – initiatives in constructing new ties with the continent. Chinese provincial and municipal officials are often the drivers for particular deals in Africa. In South Africa, for example, after 1994, it was Chinese provinces which took the initiative to establish formal links with their local government counterparts and begin to pursue business ties while the cumbersome politics of recognition between Beijing and Taipei played out (see below).[44] In the Democratic Republic of Congo, Guangdong and Katanga provinces signed an agreement soon after Laurent Kabila came to power, while Namibian municipalities have twinning agreements with several (enormous, relative to the small population in that desert country) Chinese cities.[45] The link between provincial 'diplomatic' initiatives and their business interests are apparent in Angola, where two of the leading Chinese construction firms are actually state-owned enterprises from Anhui and Sichuan provinces, both of which have formal links with Angolan provinces.[46] In the aftermath of the China Africa Summit of November 2006, Lagos State in Nigeria and Jiangsu province have signed a memorandum of understanding to promote the newly created Lekki Free Trade Zone drawing upon the successful experiences of the Jiangning Development Zone, based in Nanjing, the capital of Jiangsu.[47] Henan province has opened up discussions about setting up a Chinese bank in Nigeria. More recently, Sichuan province (which already has arrangements with several African countries) and Ogun State in Nigeria signed a US$50 million deal to build a pharmaceutical manufacturing plant that would produce, among other things, anti-malaria drugs.[48]

This proliferation of sub-state initiatives reflects the decentralization of foreign economic decision-making on trade matters, which has its origins in China's opening and reform policies in the late 1970s. Provincial and municipal authorities were given special privileges, policy concessions and financial assistance from Beijing to both facilitate foreign investment and to engage in foreign trade.[49] This allowed the growth of provincial trading companies and later enterprises, often derived from renovated State Owned Enterprises, with an explicitly commercial orientation and the financial resources available to realize investment abroad. Provincial leaders, while lacking expertise in foreign affairs, none the less used the official latitude granted to them to 'boost their own careers and business opportunities for their provinces'.[50] In this respect, Provincial Foreign Affairs Offices and Foreign Economic and Trade Commissions (established at the behest of the Ministry of Foreign Affairs and the Ministry of Commerce) took the lead in establishing contacts and promoting both inward and outward investment with the outside world.[51] The periodic tensions between central government in Beijing and local authorities, with the latter tending to 'subordinate national to local interests' in the pursuit of economic gains, introduce the possibility of these contradictions spilling over and affecting foreign policy aims and their implementation.[52] With corruption among local officialdom seen to be endemic in China, this form of sub-state engagement and investment would seem to be particularly open to poor practices and, as such, may contribute to problems in China–Africa relations.

The FOCAC, of course, is the culmination of China's regional diplomacy on the continent. Modelled along the lines of the Franco-African Summit process, the first FOCAC ministerial summit was held in Beijing in 2000 and the follow-up came in Addis Ababa in 2003. Its origins are a matter of dispute, with some Chinese diplomats claiming that they responded to an African appeal while others suggest that it had more to do with the array of Africa events that characterized the latter days of the Clinton administration, from the National Summit on Africa, the one-off US Africa Ministerial Conference of 1999 and the US presidential visit.[53] The FOCAC serves as a platform to display the benefits of regional cooperation and partnership between Chinese officials and their African counterparts. For instance, at the Addis Ababa summit China announced that it was cancelling its outstanding debt of US$1.27 billion to thirty-one African countries as well as committing all parties to an increase in overall trade to US$28 billion by 2006 (a target that in fact was exceeded). The decision to forgive the existing debt was important as much for its symbolic value – China was responding to a key issue promoted by African leaders such as Thabo Mbeki and Olusegun Obasanjo – as for its substantive impact on payment schedules. In a follow-up action, China reduced tariffs on 190 goods exported by the twenty-eight poorest African countries. With the Chinese leadership proudly declaring at the first two FOCAC meetings that its relations with Africa were 'free of political conditionality and serving the interests of Africa and China', as well as warning against the rise of Western hegemony in international affairs, the stage seemed set for a clash of interests between a complacent West and the vibrant new China.

Finally, China's multilateral diplomacy, the third dimension of Chinese foreign policy towards the continent, is closely attuned to African sensibilities. The *sine qua non* of all international politics in Africa remains the anti-colonial discourse drawn from the past. A sure sign of its continued saliency is the ability of Robert Mugabe to marshal this anti-imperialist discourse in the service of his domestic power struggle and, in the process, deflect much of the African and Western criticism of his undemocratic actions in Zimbabwe.[54] The premier institutional expression of pan-Africanism, the Organization of African Unity (OAU), was viewed by many as effectively twisting the human rights impulses which originally motivated African continental solidarity and turning them into a bastion of support for dictators and illiberal actions. The irony is that its successor, the African Union (AU), along with the NEPAD initiative, has been constructed in such a way that they have taken this solidarity notion and inverted it so that pan-Africanism can serve as a force for continental transformation away from the uncritical support of the past. This is most evident in the insertion of provisions allowing for AU intervention under specific circumstances, such as genocide, in the domestic affairs of African states. The Chinese government has a clear appreciation of the rhetorical importance of pan-Africanism to African leaders and for this reason has worked to incorporate this into its policy statements, into the formation of the FOCAC and in terms of substantive actions such as funding NEPAD projects or a new African Union building in Addis Ababa.

The politics of diplomacy and recognition

An important element of continuity between Chinese foreign policy during the 'revolutionary' period of the 1960s and early 1970s and the contemporary commercially oriented drive into Africa is Beijing's position on the Republic of China (or Taiwan). Its firm stance on the promotion of a 'one China' policy, which is predicated on eventual reincorporation of the island, and the determination of authorities in Taipei to resist this push, has resulted in a global competition for official diplomatic recognition. With over fifty states, Africa has been a battleground for Beijing and Taipei since Zhou Enlai's 1963–64 tour, and it was African votes which played a key role in unseating Taiwan from the Security Council in 1971. At its height in this period, twenty-two African states accorded Taiwan official diplomatic status, making the continent, along with Central America and the South Pacific, a significant bastion of support for Taipei. Diplomatic competition has been manifested in the form of counter-offers of foreign aid and investment, military assistance, Beijing's status as a UN Security Council member and, more recently, access to the Chinese market.

South Africa was one of those states which had diplomatic relations with Taiwan during the apartheid era.[55] When the chief liberation movement, the African National Congress (ANC), took over government in 1994 it was widely assumed that it would act swiftly to shift official ties to China.[56] The new South African government's decision to retain official recognition of Taiwan, despite its ideological similarity to China, was as perplexing as it was unexpected. Underlying this position was an alleged US$5 million donation by the Kuomintang Party to fund the cash-strapped ANC in the build-up to South Africa's first-ever fully democratic elections, bolstered by the ANC's vocal commitment to instituting a human-rights-based foreign policy which favoured support for democratic Taiwan over authoritarian China. There-after, South African president Nelson Mandela pursued efforts to promote 'dual recognition' of both Beijing and Taipei, which predictably received a cold shoulder in China and across most of Asia. Competition for Pretoria's favours reached astounding heights, with Taipei claiming it would invest US$3.5 billion in a petrochemical complex in the economically depressed Eastern Cape and Beijing countering with the US$18 billion 'Dragon City' industrial complex in the impoverished Northern Province, which would create half a million jobs and require the services of 50,000 Chinese labourers. This process was finally brought to a close in November 1996 with Mandela's sudden announcement that official ties with Taipei were to be severed in favour of sole recognition of Beijing. Fears that South African economic and diplomatic interests would be jeopardized by the pending return of Hong Kong in July 1997, the potential impact on South African aspirations for a UN Security Council seat as well as the failure of Taiwanese officials to deliver on promised development assist-ance were critical to the timing of the South African decision to recognize Beijing.

Chad's decision to shift official recognition away from Taipei in August 2006 followed an altogether different course. An ally of Taiwan since 1997, Idriss Deby's government had awarded the Taiwanese state-owned oil company the right to explore in three of Chad's prospective oilfields in 2003. Despite an agreement to channel future oil revenues into a far-reaching poverty reduction programme, a condition of a major World Bank loan to develop Chad's infrastructure in support of the country's budding oil industry, Deby decided to break the terms of the agreement once the infrastructure work had been completed. The Chadian incumbent's increasingly autocratic style, which alienated even former allies within his own government, provided fertile ground for discontent and challenges to his rule began to multiply. At the same time, the conflict in neighbouring Darfur had begun, quite literally, to spill over into Chadian politics as Sudanese refugees and anti-government forces fled over the border into Chad. Deby's own Zaghawa clan ties overlapped with those of the Darfurian rebels and his government not only turned a blind eye to their activities in Sudanese refugee camps inside Chad but was said to be arming them.[57] In early 2006, a Sudanese-backed rebel movement led by Mahmat Nour, who had worked as a security consultant for Chinese oil companies based in Sudan, began to gain ground against the Chadian government. An assault on the capital in April nearly ousted the Deby regime, which required crucial support from the French military to fend off the challenge. In the wake of these events, Deby came to the conclusion that striking a bargain with China would quell at least one source of dissent and, following the recognition of Beijing in August 2006, Nour's rebel group did not lead another major assault from its redoubt in Sudan. Notably, the Taiwanese oil company continued to operate after the changeover, however, now in direct partnership with incoming Chinese firms.

Conclusion: China rising, Africa swooning

China's contemporary engagement with Africa, rooted in its remarkable rise as a leading economic power, has been given expression through a carefully constructed foreign policy of '*rayonnement*', or overarching brilliance. By employing diplomatic instruments, financial incentives in the form of investment and development assistance, as well as limited peacekeeping and military cooperation, Beijing has put together a comprehensive approach to Africa that places it on a par with longer-established Western powers. At the same time, Beijing has gone beyond these classic constructs of Western engagement on the African continent in framing relations in terms of historical associations and ties of solidarity, both of which are aimed at distinguishing its role from that of other external powers.

The positive reaction from African governments to China's expanding presence on the continent is a testimony to the effectiveness of this Chinese foreign policy approach. The admiration expressed by African presidents, government bureaucrats, business leaders, traders and journalists upon seeing the marvels of the New China for themselves produced a public euphoria rarely experienced in politics. As a top official in Ethiopia's Ministry of Foreign Affairs gushed: 'Never in modern history has a nation successfully made such a determined and massive effort as China has in achieving progress within such a short span of time. Ethiopia has been following this remarkable achievement with great interest and admiration.'[58] In part, this unbounded enthusiasm reflects the exposure that some of the longer-lived heads of state and their functionaries have had with revolutionary China, its limited technical capacity, meagre financial resources and general austerities. For these individuals, the knowledge that within a span of a few decades China had been able to scale the development heights without compromising sovereignty, party control or engaging in the elaborate formalities of Western-inspired ODA was a revelation. The Western monopoly over development had, in some sense, truly been broken.

From the Chinese perspective, the emerging relations with

Africa were ideal, providing the economic complementarities of resource abundance with relatively open markets for their goods and a surprisingly responsive investment climate. The foreign policy dimensions also favoured closer ties to the continent, with African leaders responding well to the Chinese strategy of proclaiming that their investment was free from political conditions, and providing diplomatic support for Beijing in multilateral settings. Unburdened by colonialism and fears of its dominance (as was the case in parts of Asia), Chinese foreign policy-makers could act with a degree of apparent impunity in Africa that allowed it to make rapid diplomatic and trade gains at the expense of other external powers.

2 | The Chinese in Africa: capitalists, comrades and carpet-baggers

Though Chinese diplomacy may have instigated the rediscovery of China–Africa ties, finely spun words and declarations of intent alone were never going to sustain the relationship. This was left to China's aspiring multinational corporations, the vanguard of the contemporary New China, which cut a swathe through an African resource landscape that had been dominated by Western interests. Their ability to call upon the tools of diplomacy and development assistance enabled these MNCs to make inroads in Africa and capture markets in relatively short order. Concurrently, the host of construction projects aimed at improving access and exploitation of resources brought Chinese firms exposure to the African environment and the opportunities that it held. Their presence in turn has paved the way for the growth of Chinese entrepreneurs setting up small businesses and fanning out across the continent.

While these global enterprises operate at the sharp end of the Chinese presence in Africa, for most ordinary Africans it is these Chinese small-scale entrepreneurs, and most especially retail traders, who have had the greatest impact on their lives. Urban wholesalers and rural shopkeepers are in the process of transforming retail trade on the continent, both through the fact that they are able to bring consumer goods to market at bargain prices and by simple virtue of their expanding presence in this area. Tied to the development of Chinese small and medium enterprises is the phenomenon of growing Chinese migration to Africa, bringing new settler communities to parts of the continent.

The emerging Chinese MNC

The marked presence of China's international business corporations on the global stage is changing the landscape of international commerce and politics. Western firms, once with virtually undisputed command over the financial resources and requisite political ties to dominate global business, are now being challenged by a host of emerging country corporations, with China being at the forefront. Highly competitive and strongly supported by the state, Chinese international corporations are embarking on an acquisition drive that is capturing key resources and market share across the developing world. In many respects it is Africa, with its rich natural resources and under-exploited markets, which is serving as a proving ground for the new Chinese international businesses.

China's relationship to international business firms has been shaped by its own revolutionary past and the more recent movement away from socialism. With the formation of the People's Republic of China in 1949, Western multinationals were ejected by the new communist government. China entered a period of four decades of self-imposed isolation from the global economy. During this period, China undoubtedly built some very large companies – mostly in the energy, mining and construction sectors – but shielded from competition, both internally as well as externally, these firms lacked cutting-edge technologies and exposure to market forces. One of the earliest reform initiatives promoted by Deng Xiaoping was the designation of the petroleum sector as 'the focus of reform and model for other sectors' in the Chinese economy.[1] These entities were under the formal control of the state but charged with conducting themselves as if they were businesses.[2] In practice, this meant that they were to relate to state authorities in accordance with economic principles such as profit and loss, rather than in terms of the logic of administrative hierarchy. Under the Ministry of Petroleum, in

1981 the government introduced the first contract-style system of management, which provided for a fixed allocation for national purchase and consumption while the rest of the industry's output could be sold on the international market, where it could earn foreign currency. By 1988, Beijing had decided to create the state-owned Chinese National Petroleum Corporation (CNPC) out of the cumbersome ministerial production department, and it was CNPC's Bureau for International Exploration and Development Cooperation which became the lead body in securing cooperative agreements with foreign companies as well as exploration rights abroad. The China National Offshore Oil Company (CNOOC), China Petrochemical Corporation (Sinopec, involved in refining) and China Chemical Import and Export Corporation (Sinochem, involved in petroleum products) were all established at the same time and, with the innovations that followed, such as listing on foreign stock exchanges in the late 1990s, set the pace for the emergence of the first Chinese multinational corporations.

The 15th Party Congress's declaration in 1997 that all but the largest state corporations in key economic sectors should be privatized (*zhuada fangxiao*, 'grasping the large and releasing the small'), solidified the formation of the hybrid Chinese MNC, at the same time creating thousands of smaller private firms. Loosely based on the Korean Chaebol conglomerates, the typical Chinese MNC is heavily reliant upon political support, receives financial backing from the state and is involved in mining and energy industries or one of the other strategic sectors in the economy. As energy companies have moved out of the domestic environment, they have continued to pursue 'vertical integration' strategies that reflect an impulse for control over all aspects of the business, for instance in the energy sector, from petroleum extraction and refinery to organizing transport with Chinese firms back to China. In pursuit of the state's ambitions inherent in the 'going out' (*zouchuqu*) strategy officially launched in 2001,

Beijing is intent on 'picking corporate champions' across the range of economic sectors which, with the benefit of active and generous support from the state, are being groomed to join the ranks of the Fortune 500.[3] Roughly 180 companies have been designated by the state to benefit from preferential finance, tax concessions and political backing to 'go global' and become true multinationals.

To become successful, recognized multinational companies and aspiring Chinese MNCs have to: first, build upon and leverage their commercial success in the domestic market; second, gain access to a global supply chain through trade; third, raise finance on the Western-dominated capital markets to pursue mergers and acquisitions, which are central to their global strategy; and last, obtain management skills and technology to enable them to remain at the cutting edge of the global economy. Chinese companies are seeking to move quickly into international markets and their strategies for expansion include acquiring established brands and gaining access to retail channels as well as technology. Two approaches in particular which are typical of Chinese MNCs are embarking on equity joint ventures with Western MNCs before moving into overseas markets, and engaging in mergers and acquisitions of established companies, which allows them to obtain advanced production, new technology and managerial expertise.[4] Many of these firms, however, are venturing abroad saddled with high levels of debt and minimal international experience.[5]

An important point to make is that Chinese MNCs are in many respects like other state-owned MNCs operating in Africa, for example France's Elf-Aquitaine or South Africa's Eskom. In the French case, Elf-Aquitaine has been highly politicized, building upon or even defining France's Africa policy in particular countries such as Gabon and Angola. South Africa's parastatal (government-owned firm) Eskom represents another form of

MNC in Africa whose strategy and operations blend national concerns with those of the continent's major power supplier. The convergence between South African economic interests surrounding the hydroelectric potential of the Congo river in the eastern region of the Democratic Republic of Congo (DRC), which Eskom seeks to exploit as South Africa searches for new power sources, has played a major part in Pretoria's foreign policy calculations towards that country.[6] According to Daniel and Lutchman: 'It is little wonder then that the South African government has committed so much in the way of time and effort, as well as military peacekeepers, to the task of bringing political stability to the DRC and to ending the endemic conflict in particularly the eastern region (Ituri) of the country.'[7]

Chinese MNC strategies and operations in Africa With resource security at the heart of China's approach to the African continent, the role of Chinese MNCs and in particular those in the petroleum and gas industry as well as related infrastructure development, had become a significant feature of the African investment and development landscape. The dilemma for Beijing has been its status as a 'latecomer' to investment in Africa, as well as its relative lack of experience in developing and managing large-scale extractive projects abroad. In the words of He Jun, a Beijing-based energy consultant: 'China does not have a competitive edge over its Western counterparts in an open market. But in a closed market like Africa's, Chinese companies are able to gain from government influence.'[8] Western oil companies, not to mention industry based in other sectors, have been able to build upon generations of engagement dating back to the colonial period to secure their investments in Africa. The result has been a Chinese strategy constructed around the following features:

- *Competitive political advantage* – An explicit willingness on the part of China to work with any state, regardless of its international standing, based upon the Chinese foreign policy precepts of non-interference in domestic affairs in other states. In practice this has meant that China has been able to invest in pariah regimes that Western firms are barred from doing business in.

- *Comparative economic advantage* – The employment of a low-cost bidding strategy, centred on skilled and semi-skilled Chinese labour as well as lower managerial costs, is one of the key distinctions from traditional Western – and South African – MNCs in Africa.

- *Diplomacy and development assistance* – The lavishing of diplomatic attention, coupled with support for prestige projects and development assistance (low-interest and outright grants) in potential recipient countries by the Chinese government, is a prominent feature of the MNCs' overall bidding process.

Over eight hundred Chinese state-owned firms are now active in the African economy. For example, as mentioned earlier, in December 2005 CNOOC bought a 45 per cent stake in an offshore Nigerian oilfield for US$2.27 billion, China's largest foreign acquisition to date, eclipsing Chinese computer manufacturer Lenovo's US$1.75 billion purchase of IBM's PC business in 2004. This was despite that fact that industry analysts believed that the Chinese had overestimated the potential returns on Nigeria's Block 130, in keeping with a general sense that China is paying far above what is economically viable.[9] The oil companies are not alone in being targeted by Beijing for expansion into African markets. The Chinese government's push to create a mining conglomerate out of the 21,000 small-scale SOEs involved in coal mining resulted in the consolidation of the China Shenhua Energy Company a decade ago.[10] Like its confrères in oil, Shenhua aims to complete the transformation from backward socialist enterprise to modern global MNC and, as the world's largest producer of coal, is well on its way to achieving this goal. As is the case with the Chinese oil conglomerates, the parent company remains directly responsible to the Chinese government while its subsidiary is listed on the Hong Kong stock exchange as a bid to raise capital. In the process, China Shenhua Energy Company has had to adapt to the framework of Western-style corporations, preparing itself for the competitive environment that comes with the Chinese government's 'going out' policy. Similar processes have occurred in the telecommunications area with Huwei and ZTE, both of which are active in Africa. As China projects its commercial power abroad, strategic competition with US and European (and even South African) interests is on the rise.[11]

For a general insight into Chinese corporate motivation and strategy in operation, it is instructive to look at the much-publicized example of a Chinese MNC, in this case CNOOC, and its failed bid to acquire controlling stakes in a US oil company with large production interests in South-East Asia. Unocal, the ninth-largest American oil firm, had already come to an agreement with Chevron when CNOOC put out its US$18.5 billion cash bid in June 2005. Behind the timing and content of the Chinese bid, which was higher than that offered by Chevron, was the hope that an all-cash offer would be more attractive to Unocal than the mix of cash and shares on offer from Chevron. Chief executive and chairman of CNOOC Fu Chengyu has been forthright in expressing his desire to transform this state-owned company into a global multinational player of the first order: 'We aim to be a participant in the global industry, like all the international majors, supplying the global marketplace as well.'[12] In the end, the latent fears of Chinese control over American corporate interests caused the US Congress to introduce legislation blocking the takeover.

Though conditions differ in Africa, one can find parallels in the conduct of Chinese MNCs, especially in the oil arena. In particular, the case of Angola stands out as echoing some of the key features of the CNOOC deal. For example, the state-owned Indian oil company the Oil and Natural Gas Corporation (ONGC) thought it had secured a deal with Shell to assume the lease for Angola's Block 18, but a last-minute decision by Sonangol gave the rights to Sinopec. Crucial to the turnaround was the Chinese government's willingness to provide a US$2 billion loan to the Angolan government, freeing it from its reliance upon IMF sources (and the accompanying conditionalities sought by the international financial lending agency). Moreover, Beijing has gone on to provide billions of dollars' worth of finance, expertise and even its own labour force in reconstructing Angola's shattered infrastructure, including US$300,000 towards the refurbishment of the Benguela railway, US$2 billion aimed at rehabilitating the railway linking the port of Namibe with the city of Menogue, US$450 million towards the construction of a new airport in Luanda, and US$3 billion for the building of a refinery in Lobito.[13] In Nigeria, the promise to provide US$7 billion in investments, coupled with the rehabilitation of two vital power stations and a willingness to sell arms for use in the troubled Niger delta, was part of the package that ultimately secured the deal.[14] In the Sudan, China stepped in with a massive, and ongoing, programme in 1996 to construct a modern petroleum export industry that would serve both as a source of oil for the country and an opportunity to spotlight CNPC's growing expertise to the international community.[15] Chinese military hardware and diplomatic support for the government in Khartoum in its civil war with the South, and now the Darfur region, have played a significant role in sustaining the relationship.

In a more highly regulated environment such as South Africa, Chinese MNCs play a very different role. Joint ventures, such as the agreement between Sasol Synfuels International and its Chinese partners, China Shenhua Coal Liquefication Company (a subsidiary of China Shenhua Energy) and Ningxia Luneng Energy and High Chemistry Investment Group, to establish coal-to-oil plants in Shaanxi and Ningxia provinces, are the product of lengthy and detailed negotiations that – apparently unlike some deals struck in other African settings – are framed in terms that conform to international legal norms and responsibilities. Huawei Technologies has expanded its communications business into thirty-nine sub-Saharan African countries, including an US$800 million contract to build the infrastructure for Nigeria's lucrative mobile phone market.[16] At the same time, when Chinese firms do make headway in taking market share or outbidding local firms, their actions are increasingly scrutinized and criticized by the media and elements of civil society.[17]

The growing presence of leading Chinese construction firms, as well as smaller (and sometimes privately owned) companies, involved in infrastructure projects is a major and visible feature of China's new engagement. Concurrently a debate is emerging with regard to the Chinese practice of employing its own nationals in construction projects. The failure to substitute African workers for Chinese workers in the recent flurry of Chinese infrastructure projects across the continent, be they technicians or un/semi-skilled labourers, is an important oversight with economic as well as political implications. According to one study, Chinese labourers are paid US$1 a day in Angola (as well as receiving food and housing) versus the US$3–4 that non-Chinese companies are obliged to pay Angolan labourers, while Chinese engineers are reportedly paid one sixth of what their rivals receive.[18] In the first instance, construction firms from the West and South Africa have cried foul with respect to Chinese bidding practices and point out that systematic undervaluation of labour and managerial costs is a key differential in explaining their success.[19] Western and South

African companies argue that their legal standing in their home countries, which imposes labour and environmental standards from which Chinese MNCs are free, as well as obligations to fulfil development mandates such as training local staff, places an untenable burden on them when it comes to competitive bidding against the Chinese. Moreover, the use of nationals for labour by Chinese MNCs involved in construction and infrastructure projects, justified by Chinese managers in terms of their cost, productivity and cultural affinity, seems misguided when considered in relation to rates of local unemployment among Africans. Echoing this dilemma are the low wages paid to African staff in the mining sector in northern Zambia, where a Chinese company has reopened an abandoned copper mine, which has produced numerous complaints among Zambians (see Chapter 3).

A comparative study of Chinese construction firms operating in four African countries found, however, that, contrary to widespread perceptions, these companies actively employed Africans, in some cases comprising up to 80 per cent of their labour force.[20] While the bulk of these employees were casual labour, there are notable instances of Africans achieving managerial status in Chinese companies, though these cases appear to be limited. Furthermore, the high rates of use of immigrant Chinese labour found in the Angolan case, when compared to the Tanzanian, are said to correspond to the absolute dearth of expertise in that country. At the same time, the study declared that political rationale, reflected in the timing and targeting of particular projects with state-backed loans as well as closed bidding procedures on Chinese-funded tenders, did exercise influence: 'Often bids that would be deemed too costly by global competition standards, but considered strategically important by the Chinese government, are pursued by Chinese multinationals which then receive additional public sector backing.'[21]

Chinese small and medium businesses

While Chinese MNCs in Africa attract the international media's attention, there is an equivalent drive by small and medium enterprises into the continent which is as prevalent and arguably making more of an impact than that of the multinationals. Many of the medium-sized companies are drawn from the ranks of the rehabilitated State Owned Enterprises sector, which has been undergoing a painful structuring process that has cut it back from 300,000 to 150,000 firms over the last decade.[22] In some cases, these businesses were motivated by a desire on the part of a relatively large Chinese company to establish foreign subsidiaries so as to guarantee access to Western markets should protectionism take root.[23] For many smaller businesses, the motivation is to take advantage of China's comparative advantage relative to the African companies in terms of the production of basic manufactured goods like textiles and clothing, footwear, bicycles and simple electrical appliances.[24]

In terms of settlement patterns in Africa, both larger companies and small-time Chinese entrepreneurs have often chosen to start up businesses in areas where their Taiwanese predecessors have been established. In Mauritius and Nigeria, the links between established Taiwanese businesses and the incoming Chinese entrepreneurs have laid the foundation for, respectively, a network of clothing factories and a market for secondary automobile parts.[25] In northern Namibia, it was a Taiwanese businessman who first opened up retail and then wholesale shops, while Chinese textile firms started businesses in the Newcastle region of South Africa and Lesotho, where 250 Taiwanese businesses had already been well established since the 1970s.[26]

What is most compelling about the Nigerian case is that contact between local Nnewi trading networks and their Taiwanese counterparts, initiated as early as the 1970s, eventually provided the skills and information necessary for Nigerians to source their

47

own materials from China and enter into manufacturing of automobile parts themselves.[27] As one Nigerian trader involved in the import of brake linings and brake fluid remembers, 'For eight years I imported these things [from Asia] and saw how simple they were to make.'[28] Though only one example, this none the less echoes in some important ways the experience of capitalist development in South-East Asia, where Japanese investment, coupled in some instances with ODA, linked up with local Chinese trading networks to create offshore labour-intensive manufacturing, which laid the foundation for local industry and markets. This production cycle model, known as the 'flying geese' paradigm, holds that as factor costs such as labour in leading developed countries increase, some industries are shifted overseas to less developed countries, where they can take advantage of lower costs.

At the same time, the expansion of Chinese small and medium enterprises into sectors and markets formerly dominated by Africans (or, in some cases, Lebanese or Indians) holds significant implications for African businesses. Utilizing networks and supply chains back to the mainland, these smaller Chinese businesses are able to offer up low-cost (and sometimes low-quality) consumer products that drive out traditional suppliers. Nigerian traders who had shifted their sourcing to China – and who, along with other West Africans, are much in evidence in Guangzhou and Hong Kong wholesale markets – have felt the shock of competition as Chinese traders have moved directly into Nigeria. Indeed, the opening of three wholesale and retail shopping centres in major urban areas has produced protests from Nigerian businessmen and police action that resulted in their temporary closure.[29] Textiles and other clothing imported from China have threatened to put companies in South Africa, Lesotho, Kenya, Mauritius and Nigeria out of business, as well as forcing lay-offs in the hundreds of thousands. In South Africa, the trade unions have stated that upwards of eight hundred firms have closed and 60,000 workers have become unemployed as a result of the removal of tariffs on textiles and, after some pressure, have successfully petitioned the government to lobby Beijing to place a voluntary restraint on exports.[30] In Nigeria, more than 80 per cent of the textile factories have had to shut down and an estimated 250,000 workers have been laid off.[31]

But it is the emergence of Chinese small-scale retailers across parts of rural Africa which has both brought new goods closer to the population and, concurrently, threatened to undermine established retailers. In countries as diverse as Nigeria, Namibia, Botswana, Nigeria, Angola, South Africa and Cape Verde, the influx of Chinese trading shops has been met with a mix of enthusiasm and concern, reflecting the ambivalent impact they have on the local economy.[32] The former trade minister for Zambia, Dipak Patel, has pointed out this dilemma: 'Does Zambia need Chinese investors who sell shoes, clothes, food, chickens and eggs in our markets when the indigenous people can?'[33] In part, the ambivalent response in Africa is a reaction to the sheer rapidity and number of Chinese shops proliferating in a given area. For instance, in Huambo, Angola, there were two shops in 2002, seven by 2004 and over twenty in 2006. In Oshikango, Namibia, the first shop was opened in 1999 and by 2004 there were twenty-two shops, while by 2006 the number had grown to seventy-five.[34]

Though studies on the Chinese trading shops are few, a general picture of how they emerge and operate can be obtained by looking at examples in Cape Verde and northern Namibia.[35] An initial entrepreneur opens up the first trading shop, selling merchandise at prices at a reasonable profit, undermining established merchants in the area through superior access to supplies in China and/or exploitation of family labour. A remarkably diverse collection of stock, from batteries and radios to clothing and sundries, is packed inside the four walls of the shop, all presided over by the owner, who sits behind a counter. The success of this first shopkeeper inspires others to open trading shops, which, within a few short years, drives down the profits and forces diversification and sometimes closure. Though Africans are hired to do menial work, Chinese staff are preferred and are brought in from the mainland through legal and illegal means, sometimes being family members, at other times paying their passage in the form of a term of indenture (the passage is paid for through borrowing by the migrant, who then must work off the loan). Tightening of immigration regulations by African governments in response to complaints by local businessmen results in new strategies, including bribery, to avoid or get around bureaucratic barriers. Diversification into new businesses ensues, one of which is that of the 'migrant broker', aimed at the prospective Chinese emigrant, while others leave to open shops in untrammelled areas of Africa.

Chinese settlers in Africa

Following in the wake of the establishment of Chinese businesses in Africa is a surge in immigration that has caught African communities by surprise. From former labourers who worked for Chinese companies doing business in Africa to semi-skilled immigrants seeking opportunities abroad, the settlement of Chinese has introduced a new social dynamic to communities in urban and rural Africa. This changing pattern of migration from China to the African continent reflects historical transformations in both the political and the economic spheres in the two regions. It is useful to think of Chinese migration to Africa in terms of three distinctive waves from China and its environs. Each wave of migrants has come to Africa carrying with them interests, skills and outlooks that have shaped their interaction with the local population, as well as determining their success or failure. At the same time, the reaction by external actors

– primarily Westerners in the earlier periods, but most recently Africans themselves – has also exercised an important influence over migration patterns.

The first wave of Chinese migrants to Africa came in the late nineteenth century on the cusp of European imperialism and, in the case of the Union of South Africa and French Equatorial Africa, at the behest of colonial administrators. Seen by colonialists as labourers especially endowed with a strong work ethic, in contrast to the African population, several thousand migrants from south-east China settled in South and southern Africa and Madagascar, and were scattered around other parts of the region. Chinatowns sprung up in Johannesburg and Antananarivo during this period. Notably, fearful of economic competition, South Africa's colonial government shipped most back to China after their contract work in the gold mines was complete.[36]

The second wave of Chinese migrants to Africa came in the aftermath of the collapse of the Republic of China on the mainland and the concurrent establishment of the People's Republic of China in 1949. Settlement in parts of French-speaking Africa, including Mauritius, dates from this period. This was the height of the ideological period and saw a very modest migration from both competing political entities. The late 1960s and 1970s saw thousands of Chinese workers and technical managers sent by Beijing to Africa as part of their ideologically driven solidarity campaign. Here again, most were repatriated back to China after their work contracts had been completed, though some medical personnel and agricultural specialists remained, but without establishing much of a physical presence. A more significant long-term development was the opening up of factories in homeland regions by Taiwanese businessmen in the 1970s and, with that, the rise of Taiwanese communities in South Africa (as well as some neighbouring countries) as the apartheid legislation began to ease.[37]

We are currently in the midst of a third wave of Chinese migration to Africa. Some appear to have been labourers linked to Chinese government projects in areas such as infrastructure development or the petroleum industry. Others follow the time-honoured process of following family members to a new country and working within their established business. Another group are pursuing opportunities and have used 'migrant brokers', both legal and illegal, to obtain the necessary paperwork to immigrate to Africa. Unlike the previous waves of migrants, drawn from the coastal areas of the south-east, Hong Kong and Taiwan, these individuals are from all over China and are generally not especially skilled or trained (in contrast to the second wave). A key factor in fomenting this movement was the gradual changes to regulations covering emigration within China which began in 1974 and effectively allow anyone who can produce evidence of right of legitimate entry to a foreign country to leave.[38] Estimates vary considerably, but the following figures give some sense of this growing phenomenon.

In South Africa, where documentation on population figures was strictly followed by the apartheid government, there were 4,000 Chinese in 1946; this rose to 10,000 in 1980 and 120,000 in 1998.[39] By 2006, according to a variety of sources, this number had grown to between 300,000 and 400,000.[40] A member of the opposition Independent Democrats was reportedly recruited from the ranks of Chinese immigrants in the hope that he would draw in the burgeoning Chinese vote.[41] In Tanzania, where a few thousand Chinese had stayed on after the construction of the TanZam railway, the numbers had increased to 20,000 by 2006.[42] The Chinese community in Nigeria is estimated to be 100,000 (2006) while Ethiopia and Kenya are host to 5,000 and 4,000 Chinese, respectively.[43] Virtually no Chinese community existed in Namibia at independence in 1990 but, by 2006, estimates differed, from 4,000 to persistent claims that more than 40,000 were in residence.[44] In Zambia, where the Chinese presence has become a source of political controversy (see Chapter 3), the figures for 2006 vary wildly from the official government numbers of 2,300 to the political opposition's claims of 80,000.[45] Within the capital city of the Democratic Republic of Congo, 800 Chinese were said to have settled, again a dramatic change from the recent past, when only a handful of Chinese lived in Kinshasa.[46] The most astonishing incidence of Chinese migration to Africa may be found in Angola. The ever-creative rumour circuit in Luanda has suggested that the Angolan government planned to invite up to 3 million Chinese, many of whom would be settled in the central highlands to restart the moribund agricultural sector. With a population of 12 million in a state still emerging from decades of civil war, this would certainly introduce a volatile dynamic into a fragile environment. In any case, to date the bulk of Chinese migration has been to Cabinda province in the north, attracted by the oil industry and infrastructure projects, and the total number of Chinese is estimated at 40,000.[47]

A number of important caveats should be considered when examining these data on Chinese migration to Africa. First, these numbers need to be placed in the context of a wider global pattern of Chinese migration that has seen, for example, the number of Chinese settling in Japan rise from 50,000 in the 1960s to 600,000 in 2006. Second, the perception of Africans as to who is 'Chinese' seems to include Koreans, Japanese and many other non-Indian Asians, so generalizations and stereotyping are endemic. Further complicating the picture is the inclusion of Malaysian Chinese, who feature in the foreign investment projects in Namibia, as do North Koreans, and are therefore a possible source of what for some observers is an exaggeration. This situation can lead to embarrassing blunders; for instance, a Chinese delegation visiting Zimbabwe was greeted by signs welcoming them in Korean script, a probable hold-over from the

53

close affiliation between Mugabe's notorious 5th Brigade and the North Korean military.[48] Third, there is something disturbingly akin to racism in the singling out of the Chinese presence for scrutiny when other ethnic groups and nationalities (whether historically external or internal to Africa) have established themselves in business and settled in African countries without much local commentary.[49] As Dobler points out, in northern Namibia the arrival of Cape Malay or South African Indian-owned trading companies produced little comment from the local population but 'Chinese migrants, on the contrary, are often seen as intruders even by the people who buy at their shops'.[50]

For many Africans, the relatively sudden appearance of Chinese settlers in their midst is certainly puzzling, especially in light of their low level of skills and their apparently limited financial means. As one Angolan NGO worker put it, 'Why is China sending us all their poor people?' In part, the answer lies in the changing structure of China's once socialist domestic economy, which has seen a mass migration from the rural areas to the coastal urban regions as peasants abandon farming for more lucrative pursuits. Coupled with this is the rapid pace of urbanization, which has put an end to rural and peri-urban agriculture near the cities, as have massive infrastructure projects such as the Three Gorges Dam, and caused 2 million peasants to be forced off the land.[51] The downsizing or closure of State Owned Enterprises has produced 25 million unemployed who have joined the ranks of the 'floating population' of internal migrants, swelling it from 53.5 million in 1995 to 140 million in 2004.[52] The lifting of government controls on the *danwei* ('work unit', which tied the individual to a closely knit group of cohorts) and other restrictions on movement has meant that these hundreds of millions of Chinese are freer to seek employment outside their home region.

Another factor is the relatively new role of provincial and local authorities in encouraging emigration as a means of raising local standards of living and acquiring a source of foreign remittances. According to Pieke:

> Local government, in other words, is one of the key agents in the spread of mass emigration across China, playing a role rather similar to the national government in [other] countries, such as the Philippines, that rely heavily on emigration as a development strategy. The role of the local government is of course quite consistent with the great premium that the central government in China attaches to economic development and the considerable autonomy that local officials enjoy to purse this goal.[53]

Such locally based entrepreneurship has been at least in part behind the drive by China's provinces and cities to formally link up with their African counterparts. Promoting a local SOE increases revenue back home, provides new opportunities for local workers and new markets for traders. Moreover, having Chinese *in situ* holds out the possibility of establishing networks that can better facilitate trade and knowledge of the local market for authorities back in the homeland.[54] Fujian and Zhenjiang provinces have been consistently mentioned as sources of emigrants to Africa in this current wave, though people from Shanghai, Sichuan, Hunan and the 'rust belt' in north-east China feature as well.[55]

Thus, as one observer puts it, 'Emigration is no longer limited to a few pockets of Chinese society, but has become an option that can be entertained by Chinese across the country and from a wide range of backgrounds.'[56] For many, work overseas for a Chinese construction firm as an unskilled labourer or migration to Africa to work in a retail shop is seen as an opportunity to be grabbed with both hands. Some of these people are lured to Africa, particularly young women to South Africa, through 'snakehead' illegal migration schemes and are forced into prostitution; others through more conventional forms of illegality involving false papers and indentured work. For other Chinese, emigration to Africa is merely a way station to Europe or the United States. Whatever the case, even if only a small percentage of the millions of Chinese unemployed seek their fortune in Africa, it will dramatically change the face of the continent.

Conclusion: exporting Chinese capitalism

The presence and conduct of China's businesses in Africa are fast becoming permanent features of the African economic landscape. That this new development excites controversy within Africa and on the part of Western firms and NGOs is inevitable. Some of the concerns expressed are, it must be said, part and parcel of the emergence of such a significant economy in a liberalizing global trading environment based on market principles. In this vein, the controversy over textiles is seen as perplexing by Chinese officials, who point out that, having undergone the difficult task of restructuring their domestic textile and clothing industries in advance of joining the WTO, China has abided by the rules of international trade and the market should therefore be allowed to determine the outcome of this matter.[57] Moreover, for ordinary Africans the most significant impact of Chinese economic involvement on the continent remains the surge in low-cost consumer goods, albeit sometimes of variable quality, available to Africans as never before. These are being supplemented through the import of higher-value-added products, such as 'white goods' (refrigerators, air conditioners, etc.) and even Chinese-manufactured vehicles, which appeal to the pockets of middle-class consumers as well.[58]

There is evidence that the Chinese MNCs are, as part of their desire to emulate established global MNCs, in the process of embracing aspects of the corporate responsibility agenda.[59] As Chinese firms become more fully engaged in the international market – accountable to shareholders, adhering to governance

principles and become more socially aware – their business practices will better reflect these concerns. For instance, Chinese
MNCs such as CNOOC are anxious to publicize their social and
environmental credentials and, while no African programmes
are listed yet, they have provided donations for everything from
fisheries development to scholarships in Indonesia, where the
company has longer-standing established interests.[60] Both China
and Africa have institutional shortcomings when it comes to the
regulation of commerce and, as such, the conduct of Chinese
firms, whether domestically or in Africa, differs little. Indeed,
even critics admit that if one sets aside the particular cases of
Sudan, Angola and Equatorial Guinea, 'the rest of PetroChina
and Sinopec activities on the African continent are not especially
reprehensible', or at least no more so than those of many of their
Western counterparts.[61] Certainly Chinese business leaders such
as Fu Chengyu, head of CNOOC, are emphatic that 'China's goal
is not to overturn the world order but instead to participate in
this order and to reinforce it and even to profit from it'.[62] In the
long run, perhaps it is this drive to emulate Western 'best practice' which will be the determining factor in Chinese corporate
conduct in Africa.

In this regard, the role of aspirant Chinese MNCs is crucial.
According to Jonathan Berman of Development Alternatives: 'The
largest Chinese energy companies currently have an approach to
corporate responsibility that focuses on health, safety and environment, much like early corporate responsibility programmes at
many Western energy companies.'[63] At the same time, the OECD
report noted that Chinese corporations still lacked independence
from government interference if not, through state-owned parent
companies, outright control.[64] While the government signed up
to the UN's Convention against Corruption in 2003, it has still
to agree to the Extractive Industries Transparency Initiative and
other measures designed to instil better governance in Africa.

Far more problematic in the longer term is the conduct of Chinese small and medium enterprises, some of which deliberately flout labour and environmental standards as well as local regulations in pursuit of profit. Many African critics see the Chinese government as culpable or at least responsible for these companies' actions, not least because of its own authoritarian political structures and past. Though one can ascribe this sort of collusion to ties between the state and Chinese MNCs, this description does not hold, however, for the thousands of smaller firms cropping up across Africa. As pointed out above, these businesses are the product of provincial or individual initiatives and, in that way, reflect interests and practices drawn from their domestic experiences. The decentralization of facets of economic decision-making and the rise in local capital (to finance overseas investments) has constrained Beijing's control over the activities of its citizens. The wholesale destruction of the environment in the course of rapid development, the inability of the central government to stop corrupt local officials from selling land from under millions of peasants, the struggle to effectively implement newly promulgated laws and regulations: these are all regular features of the Chinese development experience at home. These attitudes, circumstances and practices are part of what is being exported, along with the Chinese financial capital, to Africa.

Finally, as Chinese companies spread out into Africa, and in their wake tens of thousands of migrants from the mainland, the complexities of living and working in that environment became more evident. Their presence and conduct have produced a variety of local responses, which have gone beyond the unreserved enthusiasm expressed by African governments. These changing dynamics are increasingly shaping Chinese–African relations in ways that strain the credibility of China's official doctrine of 'non-interference' and, whether Beijing likes it or not, draw China into African politics.

3 | Africa turns east

The much-vaunted rise of China has fostered an overriding sense that Africans ought to tie their fortunes to a Chinese future rather than a Western past. This appeal has been based on China's role as a countervailing force both to Western conditionalities and to the continent's reliance on Western sources for foreign investment and development assistance. Furthermore, with China's much-publicized surpassing of the French and British economies in terms of sheer size, African politicians, intellectuals and businessmen increasingly believe that the Chinese example is more suited to African conditions and can serve as an inspiration for Africa's own development ambitions. From the promulgation of Zimbabwe's 'Look East' policy to the blossoming of Chinese-language studies in Nigeria, the African continent is eagerly embracing Chinese capital, its diplomatic entreaties and even cultural trappings at an unprecedented rate.

Since China's foreign policy foray into Africa has been primarily centred on capturing the elites and the resources under their control, the rapidity of engagement has belied its shallow roots in wider African society. In a continent of over fifty countries and deeply diverse societies, the complexity of assessing how Africans respond to China's dramatic arrival is obvious. Moreover, it has taken Africans some time to assess China's interests and determine the impact on their own concerns. In order to cut through this complexity and establish some common features of African responses, it is best to look at the nature of individual African regimes in place and the underlying economy of particular countries. Three types of regimes – pariah partnerships, illiberal regimes or weak democracies with commodity-based economies and democracies with diversified economies – emerge as providing a discernible set of patterned responses to China's new engagement.

At the same time, the rise of public debate outside the framework of official ties increasingly impinges upon conduct and the possibilities of extending these government-to-government relations. As African civil society – from labour activists and trade analysts to environmental and human rights lobbies – develops a voice on the range and breadth of Chinese involvement in continental affairs, this begins to set parameters on Chinese action in collusion with African elites.

Pariah regimes

Perhaps the most common image of the new role of China in Africa is captured in the many public gatherings where one of its leaders is seen embracing a recognized African dictator. Until recently, this has been a situation that the Chinese government has been quite willing to accept, if not encourage. 'Nonintervention is our brand, like intervention is the Americans' brand,' one Chinese diplomat chortled.[1] This confident portrayal of the Chinese–African partnership drew in part on China's need to publicize its deliberate strategy of breaking into a Western-dominated resource market. But this controversial approach clearly reflected Beijing's own assessment of African politics, the elite character of the regimes that controlled the resource economies and the possibilities of forging ties with like-minded actors. How have African pariah regimes responded to Chinese entreaties?

For 'pariah' regimes China is a welcome source of stability, a new strategic partner and a provider of development assistance and foreign investment. Such states include Sudan and Zimbabwe (and sometimes Angola and Chad) which have fallen foul of Western governments and are routinely castigated in the

Western media for a host of failings in governance and human rights. Subject to international condemnation and even sanctions in the aftermath of the cold war, these governments have found that their ability to raise capital or provide for their own security interests has been constricted through an increasingly coordinated set of actions by Western governments, NGOs and international organizations. The elites within these states preside over significant extractive resources, usually in the form of energy or mineral resources but also unexploited timber, fisheries and agricultural areas. State control of these resources takes a variety of forms, from direct ownership of mines and land to licensing and leasing arrangements. Typically, the reliance of their economy upon a single resource or a collection of resources has not led to significant development but rather has served as a source of elite enrichment in the midst of a sea of poverty. Where mass poverty and elite competition have spilled over into conflict over resources themselves, embattled regimes actively use their resources in the service of security needs and to shore up support within the military. Restrictions on the official arms trade impose potentially disastrous penalties on pariah regimes.

The oil-rich country of Sudan is one such partner for China. Since 1996, over US$15 billion had been invested by China, primarily in the oil industry and related infrastructure projects. As in Angola, a network of refineries, roads, railways, hydroelectric dams, gold mining and telecommunications has blossomed across the country.[2] Tens of thousands of Chinese workers, technicians and managers have been brought in to build and run these massive infrastructure and industrial projects. As a result, bilateral trade between Sudan and China, which stood at US$890 millon in 2000, shot up to US$3.9 billion in 2005. To a great extent, Sudanese government actions in Darfur have benefited from the protection provided by the threat of the Chinese veto in the UN Security Council but, at the same time, authorities in Khartoum have felt that Beijing has not always sufficiently supported their position as expected (as the periodic organized street protests at the Chinese embassy indicate). Despite signs that the Chinese government is beginning to shift its thinking on Sudan (indicated by its decision to remove Sudan from the list of countries in which it provides financial incentives to Chinese companies to invest),[3] a US$3 million preferential loan organized in July 2006 aimed at rehabilitating infrastructure signals Beijing's continuing economic commitment to the regime. Moreover it is the hope of Chinese officials that they will be able to convince the newly autonomous southern Sudanese government, which had vehemently opposed Chinese support for Khartoum during the civil war, to award them rights to exploit oilfields in their region, a position that may raise concerns in northern Sudan should the South opt for independence at a later stage.[4]

With the Sudanese government seemingly locked in perpetual conflict, first for over two decades in the South and since 2004 in Darfur, the role of the Chinese in support of Khartoum has been under the international spotlight since the advent of forcible removals in 1998. The development of Chinese oil concessions (through their 40 per cent stake in the Greater Nile Petroleum Company) in Blocks 1, 2 and 4, which were located in parts of the contested central provinces, brought Chinese construction workers in direct contact with the Sudan People's Liberation Army (SPLA) and reportedly required them to be armed.[5] Moreover, in order to lay the pipeline, villages of the Nuer-dominated region were forcibly cleared out by the Sudanese army and militia. Increasing oil revenues from the sale of oil to China have allowed Khartoum to purchase sophisticated weaponry as well as develop (with Chinese assistance) its own arms manufacturing capacity, based at the MCM Military Manufacturing Complex and two other sites, which reportedly produce light arms, rocket launchers and anti-tank weapons.[6] The onset of a new conflict in Darfur, coming in the aftermath of the official ending of the North–South civil war in 2005, did not directly involve Chinese economic concerns in the way that the civil war had. Nevertheless, Beijing came to the defence of the regime when the US government declared that Khartoum was engaged in acts of genocide and asked the UN Security Council to pass sanctions against the regime. The Chinese threat of a veto of economic sanctions, which would have hurt its own economy (nearly 10 per cent of its oil imports are derived from Sudan), forced the Security Council to water down its measures against the government. At the same time, the costs to China continued to grow, from financial penalties for Chinese oil companies attempting to raise money on the international capital markets to the realization that its international standing was being harmed (see Chapter 4). As Abda El-Mahdi, a former Sudanese deputy finance minister who withdrew from the government in 2003, said, the country's prolonged political volatility may eventually cause 'even the investors [such as the Chinese] who did not think that it was relevant to them ... to stop investing'.[7]

Zimbabwe is the other salutary example of China's relations with a pariah regime. The Zanu-PF government, having been subject to a structural adjustment programme since the early 1990s, and in the wake of protest from urban dwellers and ex-soldiers, embarked on a controversial 'fast track' land reform of the white-dominated commercial sector. Its defiance of the norms of property law and the Zimbabwean constitution drew criticism from Western donors and NGOs, which, after Zanu-PF rigged a series of elections against the opposition Movement for Democratic Change, turned to targeted sanctions against the regime. As external investment dried up and the Zimbabwean economy went into freefall, the Mugabe regime looked to new partners to supplant Western investors and development assistance programmes. China's willingness to publicly embrace Mugabe, despite international sanctions imposed from 2002

63

onwards, resulted in Harare's official promulgation of its 'Look East' policy in 2005.[8] This drive to encourage Chinese, Malaysian and other Asian investment has inspired Mugabe to wax lyrical with the hope of winning the support of less critical foreign partners: 'We are returning to the days when our greatest friends were the Chinese. We look again to the East, where the sun rises, and no longer to the West, where it sets.'[9]

Purchases of military equipment, tourism agreements and airline connections all signalled the intentions of Zanu-PF to use state resources to secure this partnership, but China has proved to be elusive. Individual investors have entered into co-operative agreements with state-owned companies in the areas of telecommunications and power utility but, beyond yet-to-be-realized commitments to rehabilitate the coal station at Hwange, no serious financial capital has been forthcoming. The Chinese have leased some expropriated farms and are said to be a major buyer of tobacco, once Zimbabwe's leading agricultural export. The mining sector, which contains significant platinum reserves that are of interest to China, has so far remained out of bounds (though rumours persist that Mugabe has already offered the Chinese public shares and/or the possibility of acquiring some rights to the mines, but that the Chinese are waiting for the value to drop further before making any move). A prospective Chinese buyer of Zimbabwe's Iron and Steel Company pulled out in April 2005 when faced with the absorption of the state-owned enterprise's substantial losses. In the words of one Zimbabwean banker: 'Zimbabwe has literally mortgaged most of its key assets to the Chinese in the hope that it would get assistance. Without overstating the point, Zimbabwe is a desperate ally of the Chinese.'[10]

The contrast between these two pariah regimes highlights the importance of stability and, increasingly, the role of African and even international public opinion in shaping Chinese policy.

In the case of Sudan, where substantive economic interests are fundamental to the depth and character of ties with Khartoum, Chinese involvement is sustained and features at all levels, diplomatic, financial, developmental and symbolic. This is even the case after the shift in Beijing's approach to the Bashir regime, which became apparent in late 2006, and involved a more publicly – and apparently privately – critical stance towards Khartoum. As for Zimbabwe, the absence of significant Chinese investment underscores the much greater level of diffidence felt by Beijing towards any association with the Mugabe regime. Indeed, in spite of Mugabe's vocal celebration of ties with Beijing as being 'a new paradigm ... against the Anglo-American axis', the fact of the matter is that the Zimbabwean government has received very little in comparison to Sudan.[11] For instance, though Beijing was instrumental in blocking a submission to the UN Security Council that was critical of 'Operation Murambatsvina' (which regime opponents claimed was instigated to rid the Chinese of indigenous retail competition), efforts to secure Chinese financial assistance in paying the US$295 million owed to the IMF came to naught in 2005. In fact, apart from a university diploma and US$6 million in food aid, Mugabe's overtures to China produced no tangible results, and Zimbabwe remains off the official itinerary, much to the chagrin of Harare. All this has caused the state-controlled Zimbabwean media to question publicly the friendship that underpins the relationship:

> The Chinese do not believe, just like the fence-sitting Western investors, that Zimbabwe can uphold bilateral investment protection agreements and manage its economy to international standards. They have witnessed, in Zimbabwe, instances of the arbitrary violation of ... the law of property and law of contract. And unless the government realizes this, then all Zimbabwe will continue to get from the Chinese are good words of intent until

such a time as the situation in the country is deemed to have returned to normal.[12]

These examples of pariah partnerships suggest that the Chinese approaches with these regimes are fundamentally opportunistic in nature and not necessarily driven by a desire to bolster or create a 'league of dictators', as Robert Kagan claims (see Chapter 4). For the Chinese government, overriding economic considerations mandate a defence of the regime in Khartoum, especially when potential sanctions are aimed directly at their own investments, but there is not necessarily a need to go beyond that position. And, like Western counterparts, Beijing recognizes that the arbitrary conduct of the Zanu-PF regime is a threat to its own prospective investments and, when coupled with the much more important ties to a nervous South African government (and the West as well), makes Zimbabwe a pariah partnership to be maintained at arm's length. The problem of tying their economic fortunes to the fate of a particular illegitimate regime, while not identified as an issue at the time, is increasingly becoming apparent to Chinese authorities.

Illiberal regimes and weak democracies

Though admittedly a broad category encapsulating everything from states emerging from conflict – such as Sierra Leone, Liberia and Angola – to reasonably stable if weak democracies with a commodity-based economy – such as Nigeria, Senegal, Tanzania and Zambia – illiberal regimes and democratic regimes with commodity-based economies represent a governance type that displays broadly similar reactions to external engagement. With respect to post-conflict regimes, though they may nominally be on the road to economic recovery and often make claims to be conforming to democratic principles (a reflection of the donor-led bias as much as domestic commitment), the willingness to use elite control over state resources as a means of securing rents is deeply ingrained in their conduct. Equally, those states with a commodity-based economy that are democratic in character can exhibit similar behaviour, though in some cases checked by formal legal institutions or by the influence of political forces in the country. For both illiberal regimes and democratic regimes with commodity-based economies China is primarily seen as a strategic partner and a new source of FDI, though the local business sector and trade unions/civil society may be concerned about the impact on their interests. These include Angola and Nigeria, both of which exhibit poor levels of commitment to full democratic practice and have economies that are dominated by the export of commodities.

As a state emerging from conflict, Angola is fast becoming one of Beijing's most important partners, both because of its tremendous oil wealth but also owing to the investment opportunities it offers in a range of sectors. The Angolan government's willingness to open up the country to Chinese investment has meant, for example, that the US$5 billion of loans from China's Exim Bank provided since 2004 are targeted at the construction of an oil refinery, a new international airport, diamond mining and the fisheries industry.[13] Moreover, as the terms of the loan specified that 70 per cent of the contracts be awarded to Chinese firms, officials in Luanda have invited tens of thousands of Chinese labourers to work on rehabilitating key railways and roads damaged during the long civil war. Total trade between Angola and China was US$1.876 billion in 2000, grew to $4.9 billion in 2004 and accelerated to US$11 billion by the end of 2006, making it China's largest trading partner on the continent. Since 2002, Angola has become China's leading supplier of oil in Africa, providing 15 per cent of all of its imports. A further loan of US$3 billion was negotiated over a two-year period, which included provisions for building the oil refinery at

Lobito (something that the international community had been unwilling to support). A massive construction project aimed at building a second city south of the capital called 'Nova Luanda' with over 120,000 new residences along with parks, leisure centres and schools is under way, while a similar project involving the construction of forty-four buildings is being developed in Cabinda.[14] From the Angolan government perspective, the link with China is a key source of financial independence from the pressure applied by the International Monetary Fund to meet standards of accountability, and, in awarding oil concessions to the Chinese oil firm Sinopec, the Angolan leadership has been explicit in declaring its interest in diversifying the profile of foreign investors in Angola beyond those from the West. This was underscored when, after breaking off negotiations with the IMF in 2007, Angolan officials said that they had 'other partners' whom they could turn to for loans.[15] Interestingly, it was reportedly accusations by the Chinese government of Angolan corruption in handling its development assistance which caused Luanda to demote a senior party official.

As a commodity-based economy and a weak democracy, Nigeria is an important country for China on three counts: first, owing to its oilfields; second, as Africa's most populous state, because of its potential market size; and third because of its prominent political role in the African Union and NEPAD. Two-way trade between Nigeria and China was US$856 million in 2000 and had grown to just over US$2.83 billion by 2005.[16] Hu Jintao has made a point of visiting Nigeria on his last two visits to Africa, and it has been designated a 'strategic partner' in the Chinese diplomatic lexicon. Nigerian president Olusegun Obasanjo spoke for many of Africa's leaders who recognized in China's technological achievements in areas as diverse as computers, nuclear power and outer space the possibility of a new, non-Western role model for Africa: 'This 21st century is the century for China to lead the world. And when you are leading the world, we want to be close behind you. When you are going to the moon, we don't want to be left behind.'[17]

Like its South African counterpart, the Nigerian government harbours ambitions to take up the proposed African permanent seat on the UN Security Council, and this plays a major part in its diplomacy with China. Chinese investment has been primarily in the oil sector, and it was Beijing's willingness to sell arms in support of the Nigerian military action in the Niger delta which apparently secured the deal. A US$2 billion investment by the Chinese National Petroleum Corporation (CNPC) in the rehabilitation of the Kaduna oil refinery in the North, coupled with pledges of US$1 billion aimed at infrastructure projects in 2006, was an indication that the pace of investment and aid is quickening. Other Chinese investments can be found in timber, cotton and palm oil, as well as the telecommunications sector. Controversy over the role of Chinese traders has periodically erupted in Lagos, causing the government to temporarily take action against them, such as closing their main trading centres, and bringing the issue to the attention of the Nigerian senate. Moreover, Nigerian businesses, which have suffered from Chinese competition, have begun to complain about the federal and state government incentives being offered to Chinese (and Indian) investors.[18] A further complication in the relationship has been the treatment of thousands of Nigerians who, along with many other Africans, work principally as traders in Hong Kong and the Guangzhou area. Calls by the Nigerian consulate for the establishment of a 'Nigeria Town' in Guangzhou have been summarily rejected by Chinese authorities.[19]

As these examples suggest, what these regimes have in common is their desire to diversify the sources of investment, a willingness (and desire) to accept symbolic projects as part of a comprehensive Chinese aid and investment package, as well as an indifference (in keeping with their distance from society) to the consequences that these might produce. From the Chinese perspective, these economies are generally closely tied to African elites' interests, and there are fewer obstacles to rapid investment in the resource sector than they might experience in a state with stronger institutions and commitment to constitutional law. At the same time, though China may not recognize this dimension initially, just as in the case with pariah states, the weak legitimacy and poor institutions of most of these regimes may make them more susceptible to disruption, local dissent or even outright political challenges.

Democracies with diversified economies

Within the African continent, the prevailing levels of economic development and the preponderance of low, primary product exporting countries have meant that there are few truly diverse economies. Similarly, there are few fully fledged democracies. In fact, there is really only one state that fulfils in full the criteria of having both a diversified economy and being a democracy, inclusive of a well-represented and active domestic civil society, and that is South Africa. Other states, such as Namibia, Botswana and Ghana, can lay claim to this standing but do not share the same profile or economic capacity on the continent. Ironically, Zimbabwe was at one time able to claim an equivalent standing – albeit on a smaller scale – but has, as noted above, embarked on a rapid descent into authoritarianism and economic collapse. For democracies with diversified economies the relationship with China is a complex one. On one hand, China is an important strategic partner and a new source of FDI. On the other, China competes with local business interests, threatens trade unions and civil society and challenges NEPAD and South African inter-ests on the continent.

South Africa is without doubt the most important all-round

sub-Saharan country for China. Its mineral endowment satis-fies China's demand for resources, its relative wealth presents more market opportunities than any other African country, its multinational corporations have invested in China and, Pretoria's own multilateral interests in reforming the WTO and the UN present an opportunity to pursue common interests. Total trade has risen from US$2.051 billion in 2000 to nearly US$6 billion in 2004. South Africa is an influential country within the region and has exhibited a strong interest in cooperating with China, owing not least to its own ambitions to take up a permanent seat in a restructured UN Security Council. This was confirmed by South Africa's prominent role at the Sino-Africa Cooperation Forum in October 2000 and the subsequent creation of the South Africa–China Bi-National Commission as well as discussions about the creation of a free trade area (FTA).

As the continent's most industrialized country, with its own MNCs expanding rapidly into Africa, South Africa has a vocal lobby which, in coalition with trade unions and other civil society activists, has played a key role in stalling the above-mentioned negotiations towards an FTA. For South African business, in the words of Moeletsi Mbeki, 'China is both a tantalizing opportunity and a terrifying threat', a position echoed by other South African business leaders at the World Economic Forum on Africa in Cape Town in 2006.[20] Competition with Chinese firms in areas such as construction, both inside South Africa and in other parts of the continent, is strong, as it is in other areas, such as telecom-munications. An additional dimension of the South African case is the fact that it is Africa's only significant foreign investor in China itself. SAB Miller, Naspers and Sasol are some of the leading firms involved directly in the Chinese market, and by 2005 these investments came to US$700 million (as opposed to China's US$210 million invested in South Africa).[21] South African technical expertise in mining and related areas is highly regarded by the Chinese government, as witnessed by the lengthy negotiations aimed at bringing Sasol's coal-to-oil production to China and the purchase of South African nuclear technology from the decommissioned production facility at Pelindaba in 1998.

In certain ways, democratic regimes with diversified economies represent relatively difficult terrain for Chinese investors and foreign assistance owing to the regulatory requirements and degree of labour and social legislation imposed on business activity. Resistance by local industry and labour to the threat posed by Chinese business and the import of its products, which directly challenge their livelihoods, are an inevitable feature of relations as well. Furthermore, the level of economic development in these regimes may even (as it does in the South African case but not in Namibia) preclude using some of the usual 'quick-impact' prestige projects such as presidential palaces to gain the support of political elites in pursuit of larger resource-oriented deals. That being said, it is worth remembering that rule of law and contract law have not been significant barriers to Chinese investment in a host of Western countries, where the leading MNCs have shown themselves fully able to comply with and operate in these settings.

Zambia: China's 'perfect storm'

The case of Zambia, a weak democracy with a commodity-based economy, in many ways highlights the pitfalls facing Chinese involvement in Africa and the potential costs to Beijing of its deepening engagement in continental affairs. In fact, though relations between the two countries became severely strained in 2006, local perceptions of China were quite positive in the initial stages of its new engagement. This was primarily based on the Chinese decision to build the TanZam railway, apparently in response to a request by Kenneth Kaunda directly to Mao Zedong in the late 1960s, which offered the landlocked country an alternative route for its trade to that of going through the Rhodesian regime to the south. The spectacle of thousands of Chinese workers diligently building the railway, living modestly and conducting themselves with decorum, made a lasting and positive impression on ordinary Zambians as well as the political elite.

The new wave of investment in Zambia came in the wake of the decade-long structural adjustment programme which, among other measures, reprivatized the mining sector (which had been nationalized under Kaunda). President Levy Mwanawasa eagerly welcomed the Chinese entrepreneurs and went so far as to provide state assets at concessional rates to these investors, as well as giving them special treatment relative to other foreigners.[22] In 1998, the China Non-Ferrous Metal Mining Group paid US$20 million for the dilapidated Chambishi copper mine located in the North-West and proceeded to rehabilitate it, putting in place a munitions factory and company store alongside the new extraction and processing facilities. After US$100 million had been put into the mine, it started production again in 2001, hundreds of new jobs were created and, for a community that had not seen a major employment opportunity for a decade, it provided a modicum of prosperity. Along with this focus on mining came the decision to rehabilitate a textile complex 140 kilometres north of Lusaka which had fallen into disuse. The Mulungushi Textile Joint Venture, which had originally been set up by the Chinese government during the waning years of the 'revolutionary' phase of engagement and abandoned after their departure in 1994, was given a fresh injection of capital through a US$200 million concessional loan. At the same time, the launching of a joint venture between Qingdao Municipality and a Zambian company to purchase a cotton ginnery in the country's eastern province seems to echo the vertical integration strategy utilized by China in the energy field. It employed hundreds of Zambians and, through its contracts with 5,000 farmers its sphere of operations was extended to include 10,000 hectares of agricultural land devoted to growing cotton. The Zambia–China joint venture also embraced eighteen retail stores based in the country, as well as Tanzania and Namibia, and plans were made to establish an industrial park.[23] And, finally, as interest in Zambia began to pick up, Chinese wholesale and retail traders trickled into the country, building up stalls in the markets in Lusaka and other population centres.

Problems started to surface as early as 2004 when the local Zambian employees began to complain about the low wages of US$65 a month and poor safety standards at the Chambishi mine. Trade unions, with the apparent assent of the government in Lusaka, had been banned from recruiting or operating at the mine, with the result that they sent representatives to the area to challenge this breach of their legal rights. An explosion at the munitions factory serving Chambishi in April 2005, which killed forty-six Zambian workers, provoked outrage among the rest of the workforce, who were not mollified by promises (and eventual delivery) of monetary compensation for families of victims of the accident from the Chinese embassy. Strike action over wages and conditions intensified and an agreement to allow unionization was finally reached in July 2005, allowing for up to US$500 in back pay. On 24 July, workers stormed the management's offices after hearing that the money would not be forthcoming. Five of them were reportedly shot by a frightened Chinese manager.[24] Coming as this did in the run-up to an election, the event sparked a national debate over the conduct of the Chinese in the country and, concurrently, the failure of the Mwanawasa government to uphold either Zambian law or the interests of the people.

Exploiting the growing disquiet at all levels of Zambian society over the 'China question', the opposition candidate, Michael Sata, built much of his campaign for the presidency around the anti-

Chinese sentiment. 'Zambia', he declared, 'is becoming a province – no a district – of China.'[25] He made contact with Taiwanese representatives during a visit to neighbouring Malawi (which still has diplomatic relations with Taipei), where he reportedly committed himself – allegedly after receiving funding support – to switching recognition back to Taipei should he win the election. This sparked a furious response from Beijing's ambassador, Li Baodong, who threatened to withdraw Chinese investment should Sata be elected. Clearly the Chinese commitment to non-interference in domestic affairs of African states had been violated. Alarm bells were sounded in other African capitals as the conduct of Chinese business and diplomacy came under the spotlight.[26] In the end, though Sata's Patriotic Front received only 28 per cent of the vote, it won key seats and control of Lusaka and other municipalities in the mining areas, making it a political force to be reckoned with. A series of national apologies were made subsequently by the incumbent president and his ministers to the Chinese government, aimed at assuaging Beijing's sensibilities.

On the Chinese side, there was a determination to carry on in the country despite the uproar. Health clinics, an HIV/AIDS project and other community programmes were rolled out for the local people in the township surrounding Chambishi. A spokesman for the mining company declared: 'By complying with the laws of Zambia, we are confident that no problems will come to us. We will do our best to run this mine successfully. We have to keep quiet and to keep working. Why should we fear?'[27] Indeed, such was Chinese confidence that China selected the Chambishi mine and its environs to serve as one of its five designated 'special economic zones' for Africa at the FOCAC meeting in Beijing, and will be building a US$220 million copper-smelting plant. The planned ceremonial opening of the plant by the visiting Chinese president in February 2007, however, had to be cancelled for fear of protests. And, to add further to the woes of Zambian–Chinese collaboration, the once fêted Mulungushi Textile endeavour was struggling to avoid closure against the backdrop of a 'bloated' labour force, the high cost of local taxation and, ironically, the low prices of imports from China.[28] The volatile comments by the deputy leader of Zambia's newly elected opposition party, Guy Scott, that 'the Chinese are no longer welcome. They are seen as cheats and our government as crooks for allowing them to get away with it', suggest that China's activities in the country will continue to fuel political debate.[29] It would seem that events in Zambia are casting a longer shadow over Chinese relations with Africa than expected.

African diplomacy responds to China

As Chinese activity in Africa has played out simultaneously at bilateral, regional and multilateral levels, it has produced diplomatic responses by African governments that, in the main, have been uncoordinated and ad hoc. Parochial and elite interests have tended to prevail in these circumstances, at the expense of broader concerns among different sectors in African societies. The result is that the continent remains ill prepared for the dynamic growth in relations and the concomitant impact that China has had on African economies, nor have governments been able to leverage the best possible gains from Chinese involvement.[30]

At the same time, however, this general situation has not prevented all African governments from developing a more coordinated stance towards China, sometimes even in collusion (albeit to a limited degree) with other states. For instance, at the bilateral level, the South African Department of the Treasury and the Department of Trade and Industry have conducted studies of China's role in, respectively, a proposed free trade area with China, its development assistance in Africa and the trade (especially textiles) impact on the southern African region as well as the local economy, which seem to have influenced Pretoria's policy towards these issues.[31] Given the close relationship between South African policy-makers and the NEPAD initiative, the research and policy recommendations produced by Pretoria are likely to receive a serious hearing within NEPAD. The Namibian government has created a special coordinating committee to examine ways of devising a strategic approach so that the country can maximize the ties with China.[32] Ghana and Zimbabwe's 'Look East' policies, though springing from different rationales (Accra's being more explicitly economic while Harare's is both economic and geopolitical), are additional examples of explicit policy responses to China. Pressure from coordinated action by African trade unions concerned about the impact of Chinese manufactured textiles and clothing on their members' interests, as noted below, has also served to place the formulation of an 'African response' to China on national foreign policy agendas. This was manifested in over a third of all African countries signing up to the Istanbul Declaration, a diplomatic note requesting that quotas on Chinese textile exports be continued by the WTO by 2005.[33] And, as African civil society increasingly turns its attention to Chinese involvement in trade, debt and the environment and publicizing its findings, seen through such vehicles as the web broadcasts of China–Africa topics on the African civil society network, Pambazuka News, there is a growing public debate on how to respond to China.

The fact remains, however, that at the regional and multilateral levels African reactions to Beijing have been basically lacking in any strategic approach, as well as being fundamentally uncoordinated, reflecting the underlying bilateral structure of China–Africa relations. This may not always be the case as FOCAC's region-to-region summitry becomes a main event on the African political calendar and, consequently, African governments and civil society become more organized. There were already signs at the pre-FOCAC meeting in September 2006 between the NEPAD secretariat, African and Chinese diplomats that Africans were developing common positions and critiques on subjects that they identified as of Africa-wide concern.[34] These included a desire to see China open its markets to African agricultural products more readily and address the question of the use of Chinese labour.

Perhaps the most telling evidence of the shortfall in developing a nuanced and critical analysis of the potential gains and losses for Africa (though Western governments, the World Bank and the OECD have started to produce these) has been the changing nature of relations between the leading African multilateral institutions and the Chinese government. The public embrace of the FOCAC by the NEPAD secretariat contrasted with the cooler attitude of the African Union towards the grand festival that was the China Africa Summit. The Chinese donation of US$500,000 towards a health training project in East Africa in mid-2006, which received much publicity in NEPAD communiqués, was one indication of the quickening of ties between Beijing and the NEPAD initiative. Yet, while the head of NEPAD, Firmino Mucavele, has expressed support for China–Africa engagement, personnel within the NEPAD secretariat remain much more critical of the Chinese role, seeing it as both threatening to aspects of its trade and development strategy as well as to broader governance aims.[35] South African government officials have been particularly vocal in seeking formalized Chinese engagement with the NEPAD secretariat.[36] As mentioned above, it is significant that China decided at FOCAC to fund the construction of a new building to house the African Union as a gesture in keeping with its emphasis on practical support for this pan-Africanist organization. The hosting of the African Development Bank meeting in Shanghai in May 2007 is another indication of the Chinese strategy of developing close working relationships with key African economic institutions as well. In this case, the strengthening of links is expected to lead to co-financing of infrastructure and development projects in the continent between the AfDB and Chinese banks.

This increasingly overt level of support for a range of Africa's regional organizations and institutions, something that the Chinese government has committed itself to since the FOCAC meeting in 2006, signals the launching of the next stage in China's engagement in Africa. As the disputes over textiles and Darfur have demonstrated, there is a real possibility of conflicts of interest between, for instance, Chinese economic concerns and pan-Africanist aspirations. Direct Chinese involvement in African regional bodies is an approach that should contribute to closer coordination of aims such as those contained in NEPAD and the AU, as well as appropriate strategies of implementation for investment, development assistance and the management of peace and security issues. It is probable that this closer proximity will have a dampening effect on any potential public diplomatic disputes that may arise over these matters as well.

The textiles dispute

More than any other issue, the impact of China's clothing and textile trade on established African firms and labour interests has galvanized African governments and civil society across the continent. Indeed, the pressure brought to bear on this issue has resulted in significant actions by national governments and even coordinated measures in multilateral settings, namely supporting the Istanbul Declaration (see above). With the dispute over the importation of Chinese-manufactured textiles erupting in major states such as South Africa and Nigeria, as well as smaller countries like Lesotho and Kenya, the Chinese authorities were increasingly under pressure to come up with a credible response.

The ending of the Multi-Fibre Agreement in 2004, which among other things lifted tariff restrictions on Chinese imports to the United States, brought Chinese-produced clothing and related items into direct competition with African products in third markets. This was especially the case with the United States, where African textiles and clothing had benefited from special provisions under the African Growth and Opportunity Act (AGOA). The result was immediate declines in employment in the clothing sector in Kenya (approximately 3,000 jobs lost or 9.3 per cent of total employed), Lesotho, (15,000 job losses or 28.9 per cent of total employed), South Africa (12,000 job losses or 12 per cent of total employed) and Swaziland (18,000 or 56.2 per cent of total employed).[37] By 2006 Lesotho, whose economy was heavily reliant upon the clothing industry, had lost a total of twenty-five factories and 23,000 jobs in that sector.[38]

In South Africa, the influx of Chinese-produced textiles, clothing and shoes, coming in conjunction with competition in the US market, had had a major impact on local textile, clothing and shoe manufacturers. The Congress for South African Trade Unions (Cosatu) declared that 800 businesses employing 60,000 workers were forced to close as a result of the removal of tariffs on textiles and, along with the South African Communist Party (SACP), launched a campaign to force the South African leadership to take concrete action to stem the flow of losses. Coming in the context of a sustained leadership contest within the governing ANC (in which Cosatu and the SACP played a part), President Thabo Mbeki's instinctive support for trade liberalization was set aside and the government petitioned Beijing to place a voluntary restraint on exports (the South African government did not, however, follow the American suggestion to put the issue before the WTO's Dispute Settlement Mechanism).[39] Stung by the persistent demonizing of China's actions in the South African press and by trade unionists, the Chinese ambassador announced that his government would introduce a self-imposed quota of two years in duration, starting on 28 September 2006, which would give South African firms time to restructure and modernize. Ironically,

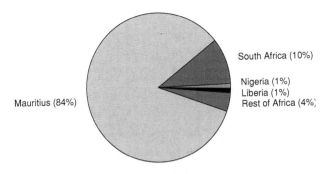

Figure 3.1 African FDI in China, 2005⁴⁰

the proposed measure induced protest from major South African retailers, many of whom depended on sourcing inexpensive clothing from China, and its actual implementation was delayed for several months.

The picture in Nigeria echoed many of the same concerns found elsewhere in Africa. Chinese imports undercut local manufactured products so that by 2005 more than 80 per cent of the country's textile factories had been forced to shut down and an estimated 250,000 workers were laid off.[41] Nigerian businesses and trade unionists put pressure on their political representatives to take action against the influx of Chinese clothing and textiles. In 2005, the Nigerian police conducted a raid on three Chinese-owned shopping centres and, upon finding illegally imported goods, closed them down. In a debate held by the Nigerian senate, politicians applauded these steps and took the opportunity to call upon China to give its own traders based in China and Hong Kong the same rights that Abuja accorded to Chinese merchants working in Nigeria.

In contrast to the tensions found in South Africa and Nigeria, cotton producers in Benin, Mali and Togo have benefited from rising trade with China.[42] Interestingly, in the build-up to the China Africa Summit in November 2006, the Chinese government

Africa turns east

launched a number of specific initiatives aimed at addressing African concerns. In addition to the self-imposed quotas in South Africa, the Minister of Commerce, Bo Xilai, announced that the Chinese government would be building up clothing and textile factories across the region, as well as committing itself to purchasing more cotton from West African producers.[43] These measures, coming in the wake of sustained public pressure from African governments, trade unions and civil society, are an intriguing illustration of the possibilities that lie ahead in shaping China's activities within Africa.

African civil society discovers China

African civil society, disparate and chronically underfunded, even actively persecuted in some countries, none the less plays a part in fostering debate within Africa on key political, economic and social issues. Generally, and in keeping with its self-assigned role as state 'watchdog', African civil society has been critical of aspects of Chinese aid policy and the conduct of some of its businesses. In particular, civil society groups have focused on concerns that China is having a negative impact on local labour, trade, governance and the environment.

According to official Chinese statistics, there are 82,000 Chinese labourers working for Chinese firms based in all of Africa as of 2005, up from 42,000 the previous year.[44] These figures, however, do not tally with anecdotal experience emerging from specific African countries where the number of Chinese labourers is clearly growing. For example, one Angolan source claimed that the number of Chinese labourers in Angola alone was estimated to be 30,000 in 2006 and was expected to rise to anything from 80,000 to 200,000 by 2008 (though as noted earlier, rumours suggest that it will eventually rise to 3 million).[45] In Zambia, figures vary from an official tally of 2,300 registered Chinese citizens to a reported 30,000.[46] In Nigeria, in the wake of the Chinese commitment to rehabilitate road and railway infrastructure in late 2006, there are supposed to be upwards of 100,000 Chinese workers being brought into the country.[47] In Algeria, there are said to be 20,000 Chinese labourers while in Egypt the number is approximately 10,000.[48] And in Sudan, the first country to host a large Chinese labour contingent (since the early twentieth century, that is), there were said to be 74,000 (of which 10,000 are employed by CNPC) in 2006.[49] This latter figure, it must be said, contrasts with the lower figure provided by the Khartoum government, which suggested that just 23,800 Chinese workers were registered in Sudan by 2004.[50] In any case, Chinese labourers comprise one third of the workforce at one of Sudan's largest construction projects, an oil refinery being upgraded on the outskirts of Khartoum.[51]

Where did all these Chinese employees come from and why are they brought in to work on Chinese-funded and managed projects? The rationale behind the use of Chinese labour for infrastructure projects has been clear from the Chinese perspective: the need to complete the work as quickly as possible and with minimum complications. Issues like the language and cultural barriers, low wages and long hours, all problems frequently cited by Africans working for Chinese firms, can be bypassed in this way. As the general manager of the state-owned China National Overseas Engineering Corporation based in Lusaka explains: 'Chinese people can stand very hard work. This is a cultural difference. Chinese people work until they finish and then rest. Here [in Zambia] they are like the British, they work according to a plan. They have tea breaks and a lot of days off. For our construction company that means it costs a lot more.'[52] Even African businessmen acknowledge these same traits as key to the success of Chinese workers in out-competing their African equivalents. As Briss Mathabathe of the Imbani Consortium (a joint Chinese–South Africa venture to expand Richards Bay shipping facilities) said: 'The Chinese have a strong work ethic, and we hope that this will be assimilated into the trainees that we send over [to China]. They also need to be exposed to the sometimes arduous working conditions that can be associated with this industry.'[53] A Tanzanian trader who lives in Hong Kong echoed this view: '[The Chinese] are very hard working. In Africa, our foundation was a lazy foundation. We used to have land, we used to have food, so people did not bother about working hard. Africans have to pull up their socks to meet the standards of the current world situation.'[54]

Trade unionists and ordinary labourers within Africa rail against this situation, pointing out that the potential development gains of Chinese investment for African economies are undermined by this approach. As one study of the Chinese construction industry in Africa has shown, however, the blame for employment practices may not fully rest with Chinese business but to some extent with the African governments that host them. For example, in Angola, where the MPLA government has not made specific provisions for use of local labour in awarding contracts, Chinese workers are playing a prominent role. By way of contrast, in Tanzania local labourers are used, alongside Chinese labourers, in infrastructure projects.[55] In Zambia the leading Chinese construction firm claims to employ fifteen Zambians for every Chinese hired, though the general manager admits preferring Chinese labourers over indigenous ones.[56]

It is not, however, just the number of Chinese workers employed by Chinese firms to do a variety of skilled and unskilled work which is of concern to Africans. Once Chinese workers have spent time in African countries, there is a marked tendency for some to stay on, either working on new projects with the Chinese firm that brought them to the continent or to branch off into their own small business pursuits. This situation feeds into concerns about Chinese settlement in parts of Africa.

The fact of the matter is that Chinese government incentives to invest long term in Africa have put in place, whether deliberately or otherwise, a de facto emigration policy. This is given expression through the use of state-linked MNCs and ODA to encourage investment in African countries with which China has economic interests, and the lack of follow-through by Chinese authorities to keep tabs on their workers. The other means by which Chinese emigration is being encouraged is through the scaling up of Chinese government publicity as to the opportunities available in Africa for Chinese business. And, with provincial and local officials taking the lead, local SOEs, small businesses and even labourers are seeing opportunities in moving to Africa. Reflecting these trends are hundreds of the thousands of Chinese settling in African countries in the last decade and half. As noted in Chapter 2, estimates vary, however, owing primarily to poor data collection on the part of both African and Chinese governments, so all figures should be treated with caution. Furthermore, illegal immigration makes these official calculations suspect.

Many Africans are pointing out the possibility that the influx of Chinese migrants, coupled with the negative impact of employment practices and other acts viewed as discriminatory by local people, could spark acts of xenophobia and racism.[57] Indeed, this has already occurred in Lesotho in the 1990s and more recently in the aftermath of the anti-Chinese election campaign in Zambia. But instances of anti-Chinese feeling prevail in many African countries, with Zambians being particularly vocal on this point. One letter to the editor of a national newspaper declared: 'The [Zambian] employees are even subjected to serious beatings due to lack of communication. They [the Chinese] can't speak English to give proper instructions ...'[58] Chinese MNCs are increasingly sensitive to this accusation, having encountered problems, especially in non-English-speaking environments. In response, they are reportedly encouraged by their managers to learn Arabic in Sudan and Portuguese in Angola.

Conversely, it remains the case that xenophobia and racism are experienced by Africans in China. This was a persistent and well-documented problem for visiting African students in the past, and one can presume that some of these attitudes are carried over in the Chinese communities taking root in Africa today. A Chinese art curator, himself raised in Africa, suggests, however, that there may be a stronger possibility of cultural affinity than suggested by racist attitudes:

> I have lived in Hong Kong for a long time, and I know that when some Chinese hear mention of Africa, it conjures up images of cannibalism, black magic, human sacrifice and famine. They don't realize the Africans and Chinese share certain fundamental beliefs and traditions, such as respect for their ancestors and a belief in spirits, and even certain elements of art.[59]

As mentioned above, the growing numbers of African traders in south-east China and Hong Kong expose the Chinese to Africa (and vice versa) in ways that may act to change these prejudices. An estimated 100,000 West Africans are living in the Guangzhou and Hong Kong region, most engaged in supplying or sourcing merchandise for trade in Africa.[60] African students or former students who have studied in China are another group who reside in the country and have sought to turn their technical and linguistic skills into employment. With few exceptions, however, African governments have made little effort to use these individuals.[61] South African firms, which are active on the mainland and Taiwan, have been more willing to employ former students with Chinese-language skills and training, as has the South African government.

At the macroeconomic level, the structure of trade between Africa and China has brought numerous complaints from concerned African elites, both within and outside governments. The Economic Commission for Africa (ECA) has indicated that it found the pattern of trade between China – as well as other Asian economies – and Africa to be worrisome, as it merely replicated the continent's traditional role in the political economy of neocolonialism. Adebayo Adedeji, the former head of the ECA, has noted:

> The traditional scenario that obtained in our trade with the developed world, whereby our country supplies the former with commodities and imports from there manufactured products including capital goods, is being reproduced, deliberately or not, in our intra-third world trade. I feel such a situation is completely unacceptable to us.[62]

Trade researchers at think tanks in South Africa have reacted cautiously to the prospects of a free trade agreement with China.[63] The prospect of a continuing influx of Chinese products that can undercut locally manufactured goods, thereby contributing to a 'deindustrialization' of the region, is taken quite seriously by governments and business alike.

More generally at the micro level, the proliferation of Chinese retail shops has brought about its own source of discontent among Africa's ordinary people. A street vendor in Lusaka captured the concern of many when he declared: 'These Chinese investors just come here to make money and take away from us even the simple businesses like selling groceries in markets. Honestly, is this the kind of foreign investment we can be celebrating about?'[64] African environmental groups have also discovered that in some clear cases China's presence has had a deleterious effect on the local ecology. For instance, the legal and illegal logging of timber in Liberia, Gabon, Equatorial Guinea, Cameroon and Mozambique (and possibly other locations) has wreaked havoc on the prospects for sustainable forestry and has even taken place within national parks.[65] In Mozambique's Zambezia province, weak oversight and regulation have been exploited by Chinese timber firms, which, in collusion with customs officials and local loggers, have cut well beyond what is deemed to be sustainable for the maintenance of the local industry.[66] Furthermore, over-fishing by Taiwanese trawlers (along with other culprits) off the eastern and southern African coasts has begun to damage local communities dependent on fishing for their livelihood. Adding to these concerns is the willingness of the Chinese government to fund large infrastructure projects such as dams which are deemed to be unsound owing to arbitrary displacement of local inhabitants and the environmental consequences. The construction of the US$1.8 billion Merowe dam in Sudan, as well as two other dam projects on the Nile, has provoked controversy for its uprooting of the Hambdan and Amri peoples.[67] In Mozambique, a recent commitment to build the Mphanda Nkuwa dam on the Zambezi in what is purported to be an earthquake-prone area has raised similar issues. This trend towards Chinese government financing of big dams has its roots in the decision in the 1990s to fund the Three Gorges Dam project in China itself after the World Bank had turned it down for its many negative effects. As one African environmental campaigner has put it: 'This low-price development model [used by China] actually comes at a very high cost – to societies, both inside and outside China, as well as to the environment.'[68]

Since the 1980s, outright criminality has also featured along-side legitimate business pursuits from China. Chinese triads have been implicated in the stripping of the southern African coast of abalone (90 per cent of which is gone after only a few years), in the shark fin and rhino horn trade, as well as in people trafficking.[69] Seven major triad-affiliated groups, four from Hong Kong (including the notorious 14K gang) and three from Taiwan, have used front companies to engage in illicit trade in wildlife products. For instance, in September 2000 South African police arrested the alleged leader of a Taiwanese criminal group who was trying to smuggle 603 kilograms of abalone from Johannesburg International Airport to Hong Kong. He was the owner of a legitimate abalone export business and had used this as a cover for the export of huge quantities of this delicacy, including well over a million dollars' worth in this particular consignment of 14 tons.[70]

Finally, some African NGOs are alarmed at the close ties being cultivated by Beijing with pariah regimes. For example, Phil ya Nangolah, head of Namibia's National Society for Human Rights, declared:

> China's defiance of international public opinion vis-à-vis the dictatorial Sudanese regime of President Omar al-Bashir is totally unacceptable. Chinese trade and other involvements with Sudan only serve to economically strengthen al-Bashir's iron fist and thereby aggravate the genocidal human rights violations in Darfur.[71]

Zimbabwean and South African human rights activists have deplored the connection between the Mugabe government and China, especially the purchase of six military trainer jets and radio jamming equipment. Linked to this are concerns about the growing trade in Chinese-manufactured arms, from light weapons to heavy military equipment, with pariah regimes and other African governments.[72] Lastly, the impact on governance issues has raised fears that the gains in asserting the right to greater transparency and accountability would be undermined by Chinese loans as well as saddling Africa with a new cycle of unsustainable debt.[73]

Conclusion

African responses to China have been in the main positive, though greater exposure and more thorough analysis of the costs and benefits of Chinese investments and ODA in Africa have tempered some of the initial unbridled enthusiasm. For African governments, the Chinese role has produced differing reactions based on the three regime types outlined above. What is crucial to understanding the varied reactions by African governing elites is their own relationship to the law and constitutional structures that prevail in their respective states. In those countries where elites have exclusive control over access to the country's resources, they oblige external actors to cultivate personal relations with them, whereas in those countries where the rule of law is meaningfully enforced, the emphasis has been on meeting legal requirements and due process.

These responses by African governments have in turn influenced the Chinese approach to the continent, as its own position and standing within Africa have changed from aspirant investor to increasingly established presence. The vast majority of China's investments in Africa have been in the energy sector, and the first impulse of Chinese officials has been to seek out easy deals that allow them to capture resources quickly, which has generally corresponded with a high level of fostering of elite ties and a low level of due process or legal scrutiny. As Chinese business has become more deeply embedded, however, their concerns have shifted from attaining access to resources and market share to sustaining their position and investments. This can be seen, for example, in the changing attitude of the Chinese mining company in Zambia, which has increasingly sought to bring its business practices in line with established legal requirements, such as allowing trade union activity, as a safeguard against popular dissent. It is significant that complying with Zambian law is now seen as a refuge for Chinese businesses rather than something to avoid or ignore.[74]

With respect to African civil society, the growing negative assessment of China's role coming from civil society activists – as opposed to Western governments or NGOs – on the issues of labour conditions, the environment, trade and human rights is more difficult for the Chinese authorities to counter than equivalent statements from Westerners. At this stage the Chinese reaction to such criticism has been to make a symbolic gesture, similar to the actions aimed at winning over African elites – financing a 'social good' such as a hospital or offering financial assistance to ameliorate the perceived problem. The announcement of US$3.5 million towards supporting the financially strapped African Union peacekeeping force in Darfur in June 2006 is an example of the latter. The fact of the matter is, however, that short of donations to civil society groups themselves, these measures are unlikely to do much to dampen down criticism.

Especially disconcerting for Beijing, and probably with greater potential fallout, is the growing connection between Chinese activities in particular countries and the use of this link by opposition parties in their domestic strategies for attaining political power. With China deliberately fostering close ties with governing elites, it is inevitably tarred with accusations of mutual collusion, if not outright collaboration with the standing regime. At the benign end of the spectrum, opposition parties in Botswana criticize the terms of Chinese loans to the government for a housing construction project using Chinese firms.[75] At the other extreme, in Zimbabwe, the Movement for Democratic Change sees the government's close ties with China as tantamount to an alliance with their oppressor. And, as was seen in Zambia, Zimbabwe and Botswana, opposition politicians are starting to use discontent with China's role in the economy, and even the very presence of Chinese in the country, as a gambit for winning political support among the population.[76]

For China, the ability and desirability of holding to its stance of 'non-intervention' in African affairs is becoming increasingly difficult to sustain as its own embedded interests are subject to domestic influences and challenges by Africans from all sectors.

The realization of the ambitions that drove China to engage in Africa now preclude it from maintaining that position given that it is, by dint of its political associations or business activities, part of the domestic environment and therefore subject to local politics. Managing this emerging and troubling dynamic is one of the key challenges facing the Chinese as they seek to consolidate ties with Africa.

4 | Between hope and fear: Western reactions to China

Africa, the erstwhile forgotten continent, is once again the object of Great Power interest. The West, architect of the African state system and its economic foundations, seeks to tie its prevailing commercial dominance to an ambitious agenda of structural change for the continent. By way of contrast China has entered Africa simply to feed the insatiable hunger of its own infant market economy, and has little interest in Africa's internal problems or politics. The result has been a new scramble for African resources, but one in which the interests of the Great Powers are increasingly taking on an ideological tint, pitting two visions of foreign partnership with Africa against one another.

For African leaders, this competitive environment has proved to be an unexpected boon, throwing a lifeline to faltering market economies and recalcitrant dictators alike, and presenting them with fresh opportunities to attract foreign capital and enhance regime security. At the same time, however, the relentless pace of foreign acquisitions of African resources and competing forms of partnership embodied in the G8 African Plan and the China–Africa initiatives emanating from Beijing have seemingly put Western and Chinese interests on a collision course.

The West's new partnership with Africa

The West's long-standing engagement with Africa, stemming from the colonial era and enduring into the contemporary period, has been predicated upon a conflation of economic interests, Great Power rivalries and a desire to reshape African societies. The convergence of Western interests, partially a product of the cold war and its aftermath as well as the integration of Europe, has resulted in an increasingly cooperative strategy towards the continent. As overt Western political rivalry has diminished (though not disappeared) and its economic interests in Africa have been reduced to a few key sectors, there has been a resurgence of the impulse to transform Africa. At the same time, a new generation of African leaders, influenced by liberal ideas of the power of the market and the importance of democracy, have themselves taken up the call for a restructuring of African economies and political systems to incorporate these values. The result has been the development of a shared agenda for change among the West, the G8 and Africa's top political and economic states, led by South Africa.

The G8 has represented the interests of the world's leading industrialized economies since the advent of the first oil shock in 1973. Through an annual series of meetings between financial ministers culminating in a heads of government summit, the leaders of the United States, Britain, France, Germany, Japan, Italy and Canada (with the anomalous addition of Russia in 1998) have used the forum to establish a consensus on the policies that would guide the world economy in a manner consistent with their interests. Though initially founded as an economic grouping, the G8 has evolved, especially in the post-cold-war era, into a gathering of political leaders whose ambitions have extended beyond that initial brief to include concerns such as promoting a market-friendly development and governance agenda in the South as well as combating the rise of new forms of international terrorism. Part of the reason for this expansion of the G8 agenda is the onset of the anti-globalization movement and its targeting of the sterile preserve of financial advisers, monetarists, policy-makers and corporate interests. G8 summits have become – along with the World Economic Forum and annual World Bank and IMF meetings – the object of intensive scrutiny and sometimes virulent public criticism as a loose coalition of anti-globalization activists has used media attention to raise awareness of the negative impact that trade liberalization has had on labour and environmental concerns in the Third World. Compounding this was a generational shift in leadership in the West, which brought into office former student and labour activists for whom the lifelong pursuit of political power has been tied to a putative transformative agenda, and who were themselves responsive (at least rhetorically) to some aspects of the anti-globalization critique. The result was a shift in G8 summit meetings away from their sole economic orientation towards a more explicitly normative agenda, with Western leaders taking up an eclectic set of issues linked to, as noted above, economic development in the South, including ameliorating the worst effects of the East Asian financial crisis and resolving the 'global digital divide'. In this setting, it did not take long for Africa's state of perpetual crisis to be put on the West's agenda.

The dire conditions in Africa, which had only attracted limited interest in the West since the end of the cold war, underscored the failings of African leadership and donor-led development assistance. Africa was often portrayed as the 'hopeless continent', and its diminishing share of world trade (less than 1.6 per cent) and FDI, as well as its unsustainable debt servicing ratio, pointed to the economic failings of post-independence governments.[1] Furthermore, brutal civil wars, the HIV/AIDS scourge and persistent famine, coupled with corrupt and venal leadership, had left much of the population mired in poverty. The overall reduction in foreign aid from traditional Western sources, even in the face of the crisis, suggested that there was little interest in or commitment to tackling the problems of the continent. With more than half of Africans living on less than one dollar a day, there seemed little prospect for improvement of their situation without substantial intervention and concerted financial support from the world's leading economies.

The chosen instrument for Western policy towards the continent had, for the better part of two decades, been the International Monetary Fund and the World Bank. OECD donor countries were, of course, through the IMF and the World Bank, already deeply involved in the restructuring of African economies. Since 1981 programmes had been targeted at eliminating market distortions such as price controls and fixed currencies, opening African economies to foreign direct investment as well as cutting runaway public spending on bloated civil service and inefficient parastatals. The introduction of so-called 'political conditionalities', namely transparency and good governance, in the early 1990s reflected disquiet within the international financial institutions that these structural adjustment programmes as constituted did not bring about the expected turnaround or increased foreign investment in Africa. This new diagnosis of the shortcomings of Africa's unaccountable leadership, persistent corruption and conflict formed the basis of a convergence between G8 and African initiatives in the new century.

At the behest of a coalition of Western and African advocates led by the Jubilee 2000 campaign, Britain's Labour Party, newly ensconced in office and infused with idealism, took up the notion of exploring the implications of cancelling Africa's outstanding debt at the G8 meeting in Birmingham in 1998. The 1999 G8 summit held in Cologne became the first meeting to commit itself to addressing the debt burden held by African states. Britain and Germany announced the cancellation of millions of dollars' worth of bilateral debt to a range of the poorest African countries. This step was followed by most G8 states, though the Jubilee 2000 campaign did not achieve its central aim of eliminating multilateral debt until several years later. At the United Nations, the promulgation of the Millennium Development Goals – a set of eight basic development targets for the continent to be met within the next fifteen years, to which Western and African governments committed themselves (along with other member states) – laid out the parameters for measuring the global commitment to improving the livelihood of ordinary Africans.

By 2000, the Japanese government's hosting of the G8 summit in Okinawa included an unprecedented invitation to selected African leaders to participate, a move that fed into its own sputtering African initiative, the Tokyo International Conference on African Development (TICAD). TICAD had emerged out of the Global Coalition for Africa's call in 1989 for a fresh approach to African problems through the creation of a new partnership for development between donors and recipients. The Japanese initiative sought to apply the lessons of export-led development, captured in the influential (but flawed) World Bank publication *The East Asian Miracle*, to lift African economies and, concurrently, tie them more closely to Japanese interests. Japan's decade-long stagnant economy, which forced upon it severe cuts in its ODA budget, reduced the impact of the initiative to that of a series of regional meetings with African representatives, a 'jamboree' TICAD conference every five years and a host of unfulfilled expectations, if not commitments.

In Africa, the idea of reconstituting the relationship with donor countries had remained alive and was to take on new form in the hands of African leaders in conjunction with their European counterparts. Crucial to the renewal of this process was the election of Thabo Mbeki in 1999 to the presidency in South Africa. His articulation of a transformative vision of an African renaissance inspired a search in South African circles for means to give the vision concrete effect. In 2000 his office produced the outline of a plan called the New Initiative for Africa, which, when cobbled together with Senegalese president Abdoulaye Wade's Omega Plan, formed the core of what came to be known as the New Partnership for African Development (NEPAD). NEPAD envisaged a reconfiguring of donor–recipient relations, such that market-led

Between hope and fear

97

approaches to development would be encouraged among African states, as would good governance and transparency. At the heart of the initiative was the African Peer Review Mechanism (APRM), named after and loosely based on an equivalent process in the OECD, which obliged signatory African governments to put themselves up for periodic review to assess their adherence to 'best practice' in pursuing democratic governance and liberal market criteria. A commitment on the part of African states to abide by these terms was to be matched by a commitment on the part of G8 countries to increase development assistance to Africa and channel it to recognized participants, including direct transfers of funds to enhance the performance of governments in critical areas such as financial management, as outlined in the Africa Action Plan agreed by the G8 at Kananaskis. The IMF and the World Bank were expected to support this process through their own programming strategies, and donors generally were encouraged to support the initiative by coordinating their development assistance to conform to NEPAD priorities.

After the Okinawa summit, the G8 heads of state meetings in Genoa, Kananaskis and Evian all featured the participation of the same group of African leaders (from South Africa, Nigeria, Senegal and Algeria) and, through that extended process of interaction, the emergence of a consensus of support among Western leaders. At the forefront in promoting the NEPAD initiative was the British government, which established the Africa Commission in anticipation of its assumption of the G8 chair in 2005. A number of key figures in Britain and Africa were included among its members. Tony Blair, who had memorably declared Africa to be a 'scar on the world's conscience', along with the Chancellor of the Exchequer, Gordon Brown, was personally committed to the transformative agenda for the continent and worked to ensure that Western leaders, NGOs and businesses contributed to shaping the programme of change through a widespread consultation process. Intensive lobbying of fellow G8 leaders in the build-up to the summit in Gleneagles by Blair and Brown, along with public awareness campaigns such as 'Make Poverty History' driven by NGOs and celebrities such as Bob Geldof and U2's Bono, culminated in the 'Live 8' concerts in a number of G8 capitals on the weekend before the summit.

Though it was marred by the July bombings in London, the G8's Gleneagles summit none the less brought together Western and African leaders to formally agree to support the agenda for change envisaged in NEPAD. OECD donors, again led by Britain, committed themselves to both raising their levels of foreign aid to Africa (to be doubled by 2010) and channelling it to African governments that demonstrated their adherence to the twin criteria of sound market-oriented policy practices and good governance. For instance, a key component of the Gleneagles Agreement was the Investment Climate Facility, to which the British government gave US$30 million, aimed at rewarding African governments that had signed up to the African Peer Review Mechanism (APRM) by reducing Western obstacles to investment and concurrently promoting their countries as investment destinations. G8 export subsidies, which kept African goods out of Western markets, were to be reviewed and scrapped in line with WTO rules, and US$40 billion of multilateral debt would be written off. Business initiatives, such as the Business Contact Group (later Business Action for Africa), have sought to promote public–private partnerships as a means of leveraging private capital in support of African development. American interest in this transformative agenda for Africa seemed at times only half-hearted (and even a sop to its British ally in Iraq), and given that the Foreign Office anticipated a diminished place for Africa in the next summit under Russia, the Gleneagles summit was felt by most observers to be a partial success at best.

Partnership and problems The new Western partnership with Africa, founded on public–private approaches to development and aimed at enhancing the role of effective and democratic African states, may have been negotiated in the North but its proving ground was always going to be the continent itself. Despite the spirited rhetoric surrounding the build-up to the G8 summit, much of which focused on Western shortcomings in supporting African development, the fact is that there was a growing sense of the reluctance African leaders to support the process with concrete action. Only sixteen countries had signed up for the APRM by the time of the G8 summit, causing the South Africans to castigate fellow African governments. As worrisome were the countries that remain outside the process, including recognized democracies with thriving economies, such as Botswana. While more countries have signed up since then, bringing the total to twenty-six by May 2006, and the process of formal review has begun, there is still no sense as to how violators will really be handled by their peers. The fact remains that despots like Robert Mugabe have received only the mildest of criticisms from fellow Africans for their violation of all features of the NEPAD agenda. More fundamentally, the link between FDI and governance or transparency practices – at least when it comes to Africa and the procurement of energy resources – is weak at best, with multinational corporations actively seeking out opportunities in countries that meet little or no 'good govern-ance' criteria at all.

At the same time, as had been feared within some circles in Britain, even the limited Western commitment to the Glen-eagles Agreement has also been difficult to sustain. The problems associated with getting Western governments and corporations to provide the core funding, pegged at $550 million dollars over seven years, for the Investment Climate Facility highlighted the continuing reluctance to take Africa seriously in the West. Donor assistance has not risen, as promised by leading donors at a meeting on finance and development held in Monterrey in 2002 and reiterated as part of the G8's African Action Plan, at rates that would meet the goal of US$12 billion per annum.[2] On a broader level, the failure to realize Western commitments made at the Doha Round of the WTO to open up the European Union and United States markets to African products, especially in the area of agriculture, where Africa has a comparative advantage, was met with strong disappointment.

Finally, Western governments and NGOs have viewed with alarm the continuing spectre of conflict, violations of human rights and undermining of market values across the continent, and the failure of African states, even through the newly enhanced African Union, to address these situations. The role of Prime Minister Meles Zenawi's government in the disputed Ethiopian elections of 2006 was especially distressing from the Western perspective, as he had been a member of Britain's Africa Commission and deeply involved in the whole G8–Africa partnership process. The initial paralysis and subsequent failure of the African Union to halt ethnic cleansing in the Darfur region of Sudan is another case in point. Chad's wilful ignoring of binding agreements with the World Bank to distribute part of its oil windfall for development in exchange for a loan, coupled with Robert Mugabe's assault on Zimbabwean democracy, is a pointed divergence from the NEPAD spirit.

As these serious obstacles to realizing the G8's Africa ambitions have emerged, China's resoundingly successful diplomacy and penetration of Africa economies have come under increasing scrutiny. What has been deeply troubling for the West is that the role that China is playing is predicated on being seen as an alternative source of foreign investment and diplomatic support for African governments weary of all manner of Western interference. As Deputy Foreign Minister Zhou Wenzhong declared forthrightly in 2004: 'You [the West] have tried to impose a market economy and multiparty democracy on these countries which are not ready for it. We are also against embargos, which you have tried to use against us.'[3] The disturbing character of China's 'no conditionalities' was that it succeeded in capturing African elites with ease, irrespective of their lack of democratic credentials. The directness of the Chinese challenge to the G8 vision for partnership and transformation is only just taking root.

The Chinese challenge to the West in Africa

At the height of the European 'scramble for Africa' in the late nineteenth century, competing French and British military contingents racing to claim territory in Sudan nearly clashed over a hamlet called Fashoda, provoking a major diplomatic crisis. Over a hundred years later, the West and China find themselves at odds in the Sudan with their competing economic interests and differing visions of partnership with Africa fuelling diplomatic actions that, like their predecessor, hold wider ramifications. For the West, the meteoric rise of Chinese interests in Africa has raised uncomfortable questions as to its own ability to retain pre-eminence in the economic and political spheres on the continent. In particular, Chinese inroads into Africa have raised questions as to the utility of the West's campaign to systematically restructure the economic and political life of the continent.

In the economic sphere, the presence and conduct of China's businesses in Africa are fast becoming permanent features of the African economic landscape. Much to their consternation, traditional Western actors are finding that their once undisputed influence and dominance of Africa are being challenged by aggressive Chinese multinational corporations in collusion with the Chinese state. As the president of the Corporate Council on Africa, a US industry lobby group based in Washington, DC, worries, 'By American companies not taking more initiative in Africa, we're going to lose important market share to the Chinese.'[4] The loss of lead-operator rights to an oil block to a joint venture by Sinopec–Sonangol is attributed by some in the oil industry to the French government's persecution of its nationals, in particular Jean-Christophe Mitterrand, who had been involved in the covert 'arms for oil policy' during the Angolan civil war.[5] Western firms have also lost out on infrastructure contracts to Chinese bids and, more generally, the low-cost Chinese products have crowded out Western producers in all but the small upper-end or luxury market in Africa. Part of the problem facing Western business is the 'good governance' agenda that its governments have sought to promote, embedded in African initiatives such as NEPAD and the African Union, which is increasingly seen as a liability by African and Western firms alike. As the head of Nigeria's Investment Promotion Commissions says, 'The US will talk to you about governance, about efficiency, about security about the environment. The Chinese just ask: "How do we procure this license?"'[6]

The complexity – or potential complexity – of signing up to a business deal with Western firms pales against the relative simplicity of coming to an arrangement with the Chinese. As noted economist Jeffrey Sachs says, 'China has a very pragmatic approach [to Africa]. It gives fewer lectures and more practical help.'[7]

For the Chinese government, having spent decades listening to Westerners preach about the virtues of the market, the sudden reversals experienced by Western companies and the accompanying criticism by their governments invokes bemusement. As China's deputy foreign minister put it:

In recent years, China has imported some thirty million tons of oil from Africa annually. I don't understand why this amount of thirty million tons has made some people anxious and caused them to say that 'China has taken away resources from Africa'. There are other countries that imported a hundred million tons of oil from Africa, and we have not said anything.[8]

Moreover, the frenzy over Chinese involvement in Africa has caused many observers to neglect the continuing significance of Western economic engagement. For example, while China's two-way trade with Africa was US$50.5 in 2006, it fell short of Africa's trade with the United States, which stood at US$71.1 billion in 2006.[9] Moreover, the United States has provided US$51.2 billion in bilateral aid since 1960.[10]

In fact, what concerns Western business is the ability of Chinese firms to readily call upon diplomacy and financial incentives in the form of concessionary loans or grants, as well as public works projects, in support of their business initiatives. Moreover, they are not hampered by a cumbersome need, however well meaning, to introduce human rights or environmental monitoring issues into any business deal.

In the political sphere, the dilemma confronting Western governments is how to successfully preserve their countries' economic interests without undermining the structures and emerging institutions that, at least in their view, are crucial to building successful market economies within the framework of a liberal constitutional state in Africa. China's aversion to the promotion of the latter is clearly a challenge to this agenda. European development agencies like the UK Department for International Development, as well as its counterparts in Germany and Switzerland, have all held discussions and commissioned research into the potential disruptive effect that Chinese foreign policy holds for their programmes in Africa. Similarly, the American Council on Foreign Relations, which released a policy paper on Africa in late 2005, has warned of the implications that China holds for US foreign policy interests on the continent (see below). Finally, for

Western NGOs, nurtured in the post-cold-war environment where promotion of democracy and human rights has been a standard guide for their actions in Africa, the emergence of an external power which commands significant resources and deliberately forswears any interest in this transformative agenda is deeply troubling.

It is for this reason that Chinese involvement in Africa has sparked talk in the West of an emerging 'Beijing consensus' on the continent which could counter the precepts of the heretofore unchallenged 'Washington consensus'.[11] The latter involves, of course, the imposition of conditionalities by the World Bank, IMF and donors which include restrictions on macroeconomic policy, reductions in public spending and commitments to transparency as well as, in some cases, the holding of democratic elections by African governments. The Beijing consensus, predicated upon non-interference in domestic affairs of states and the promotion of sovereign integrity, has great appeal for many African leaders who resist Western actions aimed at economic or political reform of their regimes. Moreover, the attractiveness of the Chinese model of development, which enabled rapid development to occur without challenging single-party rule, is undeniable for these autocrats. Respected Western analysts like Robert Kagan have gone so far as to voice the opinion that Chinese foreign policy, along with that of Russia, is in the process of developing 'an informal league of dictators' in Africa and Central Asia that serves as a counterweight to liberal interests traditionally associated with the West and its global institutions.[12]

The West and China: competition, confrontation or cooperation?

The United States, the world's superpower and the largest investor in Africa, finds much that is troubling in China's new role in the continent. Moreover, Chinese aims are not viewed exclusively from the perspective of the country's actions in Africa but through the wider prism of global strategic politics. As one State Department official declared at a public hearing held by the US Congress:

> China is playing an increasingly influential role on the continent of Africa and there is concern that the Chinese intend to aid and abet African dictators, gain a stranglehold on precious African natural resources, and undo much of the progress that has been made on democracy and governance in the last 15 years in African nations.[13]

The Pentagon, for example, remains alert to changes in Chinese strategy and military capabilities, noting the Chinese government's concern over tenuous supply lines from Middle Eastern and African sources of oil through the Straits of Malacca.[14] Congress itself has played a persistent and vocal part in raising concerns over Chinese support for the Sudanese government over the Darfur issue. Senator Jack Danforth, who played a key role in the resolution of the Sudanese civil war between North and South, has sponsored resolutions in the US Congress which have been highly critical of Beijing's conduct. Echoing this are the public and private debates within the Bush administration critical of Chinese inaction on the UN Security Council. With the growing constituency of support arguing for immediate international measures to halt the destruction in Darfur taking hold, in many ways the Sudan issue has become the symbol of China's activities in Africa.

This trend towards public scrutiny of China's role in the last few years has been building and has produced two sets of responses in Washington. One, promoted by the Heritage Foundation, suggests that China's role is undermining Western economic interests as well as its attempts to inculcate democratic principles in Africa and needs to be actively countered.[15] Another response, while also cautionary on certain aspects of Chinese engagement, sees the possibility of Western cooperation with China in Africa, with the influential Council on Foreign Relations and Center for Strategic and International Studies calling for a dialogue over Africa in their 2005 reports.[16]

Since late 2006, however, the abrasive language of confrontation has been replaced by talk of common interests and outlooks on key African issues between the USA and China. In part this reflects an appreciation of the strengths of a coordinated diplomacy, seen most readily in the construction of the UN Security Council Resolution 1725 on Somalia passed in January 2007.[17] Moreover, the US special envoy on Sudan, Andrew Natsois, declared after a four-day visit to Beijing in advance of Hu Jintao's 2007 Africa tour: 'Our policy and the Chinese policy [on Darfur/Sudan] are closer than I realized they were, and I think the Chinese are going to play an increasingly important role in helping us to resolve this.'[18]

The British reaction to the growing Chinese role in Africa has been marked by an official dialogue based on concern over some of its activities all the while fed by media determined to stoke the fires of controversy. Within policy-making circles in Britain, the attitude of acceptance of China's standing as a key player in Africa (and on the world stage) informs a more nuanced approach towards Beijing than those of some of its partners. This was reflected as early as 2005, when China was the only non-G8 country invited to Gleneagles as an official observer to what Blair and Brown hoped would be the signature G8 commitment to Africa.[19] In fact, London has been actively pursuing a policy of 'constructive engagement' with China, hoping to influence Beijing to adopt the outlook and policies that conform to recently ascribed Western 'best practice' on development and investment. Jack Straw's speech before the Nigerian parliament in February 2006, presenting an overview of British policy towards Africa in the run-up to Gleneagles, was an important signal of London's intentions to draw China into Western approaches rather than overtly criticize it:

> China's engagement in Africa is good news ... What matters to us is not the fact but the manner of China's engagement in Africa. We want that engagement to support the agenda which President Obasanjo and the African Union set out for this continent: support for democratic and accountable governance, for transparent business processes, for economic growth and effective poverty reduction, for human rights and the rule of law. We will work closely with China to that end.[20]

In this same spirit, British officials have been seeking Chinese help with problem areas from which London is excluded, such as Zimbabwe and Sudan.[21] As one British official said:

> There is a big role for China [in Africa]. It has huge influence in Sudan. It has been helpful so far but we have urged it, through prime ministerial and other high level contacts, to do more. We want it to press Sudan not to carry out further bombing in Darfur and to play its part in renewing the political process and helping the expansion of the peacekeeping force.[22]

Despite this, it would be a mistake to completely dismiss lingering British fears over its constructive engagement, however, as the statements made by the head of the Department for International Development (DfID), Hilary Benn, in February 2007 implied. Parliamentary meetings in 2006 and 2007 have also reflected these concerns.

With respect to France, official ambivalence and 'sangfroid' disguise a fierce debate within the French policy-making establishment as to the meaning and implications of the Chinese role in Africa. The media most accurately reflect the perspective of concern in French society, which sees in Chinese engagement in its traditional sphere of influence (the '*pré-carré*', literally backyard) as both a challenge to French pre-eminence in Africa and, more gloomily, a clear sign that its own days of big-power grandeur are fast slipping away. As some point out, the level of Chinese investment and interest in francophone Africa remains considerably lower than in anglophone or lusophone regions (with the exception of Gabon and Cameroon[23]), but this may reflect what has always been an underlying problem for French policy – that is, that their former colonies were never especially economic as resource providers or markets.[24]

The apparent confusion being experienced by French policy on the question of China in Africa cuts to the heart of the larger foreign policy dilemma facing Paris, which seeks to retain independence of action in certain spheres while benefiting from the greater power projection possibilities of a cohesive EU foreign policy.[25] The 2007 election of Nicolas Sarkozy, following a campaign debate that included discussion of China and Darfur, has brought Chinese involvement in Africa to the forefront of French diplomacy. With leading French companies losing contracts to Chinese firms, as has been the case with ELF (now Total) to Sinopec in Angola in 2005 and with a Franco-Brazilian iron ore consortium to CEMEC in Gabon in 2006,[26] and French diplomacy being nudged aside in N'Djamena and Dakar, it is clear that Paris will continue to face difficulties with the Chinese presence.

Germany, another significant investor in Africa with a colonial past, has sought to respond in a form that is similar to Britain's. In contrast to Paris, Berlin seems more reconciled to the constraints and opportunities inherent in the collective diplomacy of the EU. As the chair of the G8 and holding the EU presidency in 2007, the German government is – like Britain in 2005 – in a unique position to employ these high-profile settings to shape the China–Africa debate. One clear policy approach that it has adopted is to insert Africa into the EU–China dialogue process as well as retaining this area as a topic for consideration by the G8.

Finally, as a resource-poor industrialized country, Japan has felt compelled to keep a close watch on the patterns of Chinese investment across the continent.[27] As with that of other Western powers, Japanese FDI into Africa has been limited to a few sectors dominated by energy and other extractive resources. By way of contrast, its foreign aid programme has been one of the consistently largest (if not without some controversy over tied aid in the past), reflecting a humanitarian impulse, the foreign aid lobby (with its connections to business interests) within Japan and long-standing diplomatic concerns.[28] On this latter front, African support for a Japanese bid to gain a permanent seat on the UN Security Council has been seen as crucial by the Japanese Ministry of Foreign Affairs. The fiftieth anniversary of the Afro-Asian Solidarity Organization held at Bandung in 2005 was another bellwether of the new China–Africa relationship and a sign that Japan, which had played an important if understated role in financing South–South cooperation in the past, was in danger of being publicly overshadowed by China. The staunch resistance by Beijing to Tokyo's UN aspirations has given some pause to those critical of what has been characterized as 'anti-Chinese' sentiment among Americans. Informing the Japanese attitude is the memory of the Western response to its own rise to power in the 1980s, when 'Japan-bashing' became a regular feature of domestic politics in capitals such as Washington and Paris. Such is the impact of China that there has even been talk in some Japanese circles of folding initiatives like TICAD, which has limped along since its inception in 1993, into the FOCAC process.

NGOs and INGOs It is not only Western governments which articulate concern about China's role in Africa. It is NGOs and intergovernmental organizations such as the OECD, the World Bank and the European Development Bank which reflect the sharp sense of 'shock and awe' felt in policy-making circles. For Western NGOs, the surge of concern about China in Africa has been sudden and unexpected. Focused for decades on the certitudes of Western dominance of the African continent and, as a consequence, building their work around a position of critical engagement with Western and African governments on development issues, NGOs have found China's appearance to be both disturbing and unwelcome. This is especially the case coming in the wake of NGO achievements in convincing Western governments and corporations to support development and investment, respectively, built on principles of good governance and transparency, albeit with the collusion of like-minded African governments (see Chapter 3). China's willingness to publicly parade its policy of 'no conditions' has challenged the international consensus on governance and development agreed upon at Gleneagles just as it was on the point of being implemented. The obvious damage to this consensual position first became clear to NGOs based in the Sudan, where the Darfur crisis had provoked an outcry in the West while it was studiously ignored by China. Global Witness, for whom criticism of the Bretton Woods institutions had been a staple in the past, was reduced to sending a letter to the World Bank and the IMF in 2005 to protest about the lack of public disclosure in the procurement process in the Chinese US$2 billion loan to Angola.[29] Human Rights Watch petitioned Hu Jintao himself in an open letter published in major international newspapers on the occasion of the president's visit to Sudan in January 2007.

What was perhaps most disturbing for NGOs was that the Chinese were impervious to their entreaties: unlike their Western counterparts, no Chinese embassy officials felt compelled to hold meetings with Oxfam or the like on the human rights implications of their ODA policy. As an American environmentalist admits: 'We don't have leverage here like we do elsewhere;

we can't put pressure directly on the Chinese government, and neither can Chinese NGOs.'[30] Furthermore, many Africans seemed to relish the visible frustration experienced by NGOs, pointedly telling them that judgements about China's actions in Africa should be made by Africans without reference to their erstwhile NGO friends.[31] Africans believe that Westerners have no right to declaim on what China's interests may be in Africa and, furthermore, how Africans should react to this 'foreign' (i.e. non-Western) intrusion. Frustrated and fearful of their growing irrelevance, many Western NGOs lurched between vocal outrage at Chinese collusion with nefarious regimes and groping around for an approach that would gain them access to Chinese policy-making.

By way of contrast, there was a much more sober response on the part of Western-dominated intergovernmental organizations. For instance, the Development Advisory Committee of the OECD has commissioned research into the trade implications of China and India for African development, which points to a rather mixed picture of the relationship between Asian 'drivers' and African economies. In the main, this influential research has highlighted how the structure of trade between the two regions replicates the classic patterns of the past in that it remains an exchange of African primary products for finished manufactured goods from Asia.[32] Opportunities presented by the rise in commodity prices are offset by the spectre of the 'Dutch disease' (the tendency for rises in commodity prices to crowd out other economic activities in commodity-based economies) and the lack of competitiveness of the limited African industry in place. Additional studies funded by Britain's DfID and the World Bank come to much the same conclusions.[33]

At the same time, a debate has begun within these institutions as to how to address the impact of cheap Chinese credit, which is driving national governments intent on securing finance for sometimes environmentally or social dubious projects (as well as those that are excluded owing to sanctions) into the arms of Chinese financiers.[34] Philippe Maystadt, head of the European Investment Bank and Hilary Benn, of Britain's DfID have both indicated that some of the prevailing restrictions on international lending institutions should be reconsidered.[35] By way of contrast, Paul Wolfowitz, former head of the World Bank, was strongly critical of the Chinese role in, for instance, Chad, where a carefully negotiated loan aimed at ensuring that a portion of resources would be diverted to poverty reduction had been summarily scrapped by the government. A further concern is that this new raft of Chinese loans is undermining the drive aimed at moving away from saddling poor countries with high levels of debt. The notion that the long-standing negotiations towards the Highly Indebted Poor Countries Initiative was being undercut by 'rogue lending', in the words of officials at the US Treasury, has worried Western governments and debt campaigners alike. Moreover, there is a potential backlash against pursuing additional debt cancellations by Western donors and multilaterals if these measures merely open up opportunities for new lending from China. These topics featured in the discussions at the inaugural US–China Strategic Economic Dialogue in December 2006.[36]

An unexpected constraint on unfettered action by China came in the form of the Western stock exchanges where Chinese MNCs intent on raising capital have increasingly been listing. American jurisdiction over companies that list on the US stock exchange, based on an interpretation of the Alien Tort Claim Act, was used by human rights groups to mobilize support that ultimately led the Canadian oil company, Talisman Energy, to sell its 25 per cent share in GNPOC in March 2003. Chinese oil interests were seriously interested in a listing on Wall Street themselves, and in 2000 prepared for an initial public offering which was expected to raise US$10 billion; publicity generated by human rights activists, however, forced a withdrawal of CNPC and a restructuring to create a subsidiary, PetroChina, that explicitly denied that any of the capital raised would go to Sudan and, in the end, was able to raise only US$300 million.[37] More recently, the pressure by US-based large pension funds and endowments to divest from companies that do business in Sudan has denied funds to Chinese firms with interests there.[38] This exposure of leading Chinese MNCs to international pressure, while not to be overstated, none the less introduces a new element in Chinese foreign policy calculations.

Finally, Chinese government officials have increasingly realized that they were not immune to the classic risks of operating in the African environment, such as corruption by African partners or some of their own companies. The fact that the Chinese discovered that some of their funding support to Angola was being siphoned off forced the Angolan president to remove a senior MPLA official in charge of managing the Chinese loan and establish an office under General Kopelipa, the president's military advisor, to monitor the Chinese aid disbursements, an experience that Western veterans of Angola would be familiar with. In another echo of this concern, the Chinese government sent a large delegation to Zambia in 2005 to discuss ways of combating corruption in their aid and business dealings.[39]

The changing international context of China's Africa policy

Part of the reason that there has been a shift in attitude towards China in Africa on the part of some Western governments has much to do with changes in the international system and the accompanying impact that these have had on China's perception of its role in world affairs. Most important of these was China's admission to the WTO in 2001, which was seen by many to be a turning point in its acceptance of the Western-based international economic system.[40] Concurrent with the laboured decision-making and numerous commitments that went into securing entry into the liberal trading regime was the launching by one of the Chinese government's top economic reformers, Zhu Ronji, of the 'going out' strategy that same year, aimed at turning Chinese SOEs into world-class multinational companies (see Chapter 2).[41] Resplendent with foreign reserves and determined to use the WTO framework to project China's growing economic power, the Chinese state was equally concerned that the resources needed to both keep it internationally competitive and sustain the development drive were readily available. And finally, the public embrace of capitalists as one of the 'three represents' within the Chinese Communist Party was aimed at solidifying its domestic base as the state moved into this unknown territory with its potential for disruption at home and abroad.

In foreign policy terms, these events and decisions gave a new set of imperatives to China's international engagement. With its rapid growth and new-found international power spurring the kind of international commentary, especially in the West, that could fuel everything from protectionism to military competition, China's leaders felt the need to redefine their alarming international image. The coining of the 'peaceful rise' (*heping jueqi*) discourse followed in 2003 (and subsequently evolved into a dualistic emblem of 'peaceful development' and a 'harmonious society'), claiming that China's development into a global power, in contrast to the historical precedents of Germany, Japan and the United States, would not invariably lead to stiff competition and war.[42] Coupled with this international publicity offensive was a renewed commitment to active multilateralism, which went beyond the defensive positioning that characterized nearly all of China's actions in, for example, the UN Security Council since it took over the seat in 1971. In terms of contributions to UN peacekeeping China shot up from forty-sixth to fourteenth in the ranks of states providing troops.[43] Its conduct in the multilateral economic institutions, especially its closely monitored compliance with the WTO, had introduced significant changes to its own policies and practices. Pearson has gone so far as to declare that 'The extensive adoption by China of the norms and rules of the international economic regime would seem to indicate the success of the [West's] engagement policy.'[44]

Furthermore, the sense within China of the need to ameliorate the worst features of rapid economic growth at home, seen for example in the call for greater corporate social responsibility and a 'greener China', has its echo in the foreign policy arena. The comments of Wang Xiaodong, economist and author of *Chinese Nationalism under the Shadow of Globalization*, suggest disquiet with a foreign policy shackled by economic interests alone:

> We can't be a country that just does business. We must develop relationships besides economic and trade ties with other countries – including stronger military projection. But for the majority of the people [in China], all they want to do is to develop the economy, and for them, anyone who thinks of anything else is foolish.[45]

In this regard, the call by US Deputy Secretary of State Robert Zoellick for China to play a role as a 'responsible stakeholder', made during a visit in 2005 and widely commented on, seems to have influenced Chinese authorities.[46] This apparent acceptance by American authorities of China's international standing, as opposed to the discourse of threats, has contributed to an awareness of the possibilities of global leadership and a greater willingness to be involved in multilateral activism.

It was in this context that China's actions in Africa commanded attention and, increasingly, the Western and African focus has fallen on China's role in conflict-ridden Sudan. This brought about debate within Chinese circles as to the efficacy of maintaining links with pariah regimes which attracted negative

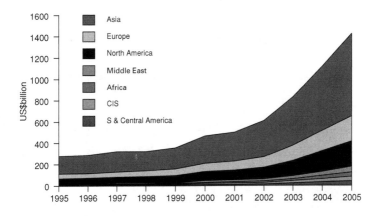

Figure 4.1 China trade by regions (1995–2005)[47]

publicity that hurt China's carefully nurtured position – born of the admonishments of Deng Xiaoping – as a quiet international player with only selective engagement in global issues and one acting in concert with Southern interests.[48] In keeping with Western support for measures taken by Beijing after North Korea's announcement of a nuclear test to bring Pyongyang back to the negotiating table and end its nuclear programme, Western governments are hoping that Beijing can play a constructive part in bringing pressure to bear on Khartoum. The first concrete signs that this new approach was bearing fruit could be seen in November 2006, when the Chinese ambassador to the UN, Wang Guangya, played a key role in convincing the Khartoum regime to accept a hybrid AU–UN mission in Darfur.[49] Furthermore, China's new diplomatic assertiveness was reflected in its willingness to lead the push by Security Council members to promote foreign intervention in the conflict in neighbouring Somalia. Wang explained: 'I was reluctant to take this role but there was a lack of interest (in the Somalia conflict) by the other major powers.'[50] Significantly, it was at the behest of African states that China was propelled into this specific action; it would not have taken place at all, however, if it weren't for the positive environment and its reception by fellow UN Security Council members. The process of bringing China into the fold of leading global powers is in full swing and Africa is one of its proving grounds.

Conclusion

China's renewed focus on Africa, coupled to its ability to make significant inroads into the continent in such a short period, is an important harbinger of change in the international system. For alarmists in the West, China's presence is yet another signal that Western pre-eminence on the world stage is weakening. The shadow boxing over the Darfur issue between Beijing and Washington, while rooted in the local dynamics of the Sudan crisis and the ongoing ethnic cleansing, none the less carries with it dimensions of global rivalry over influence and access to vital energy resources. The difficulty that Western governments, businesses and NGOs have in contesting China's 'no conditions' diplomacy, especially in the uncertain terrain of partially consolidated democracies, not to mention outright dictatorships, seems to suggest that the Western approach to African partnership is bound to fail. Or that pressure to pursue commercial interests, and most especially the procurement of energy resources, will cause the West to quietly abandon much of the substance of its continental restructuring agenda.

In the end, however, it was not so much Western criticism as the rising tide of African disquiet drawn from the reactions of elements in civil society and even some governing elites which put Beijing on the defensive. The first notable expression of this was the issuance of its first ever public statement on foreign policy in Africa. Unveiled across the continent in January 2006, it essentially reiterated the established diplomatic aims of the Chinese and its accomplishments in fostering trade and development over the last ten years. This was followed by three high-profile visits by Chinese leaders to the continent which sought to secure further resource deals (such as the US$2.27 billion oil lease in Nigeria), expand Chinese ODA and investment (such as the US$2 billion loans for infrastructure development in Nigeria) and, concurrently, assure African leaders of Beijing's enduring commitment to the continent. In particular, Chinese officials were anxious to ensure that the upcoming meeting of the China Africa Summit to be held in November 2006 in Beijing remained a public showpiece of good relations between the two regions. It was to be there that the process of consolidating its economic and diplomatic gains in Africa would begin in earnest.

Between hope and fear

5 | Consolidating China–Africa relations

'China cannot just come here and dig for raw materials and then go away and sell us manufactured goods.' Thabo Mbeki, South African president, Cape Town, December 2006[1]

'China has never imposed its will or unequal practices on other countries and will never do so in the future. It will certainly not do anything harmful to the interests of Africa and its people. China respects the political systems and paths to development independently adopted and pursued by the African people that suit their national conditions.' Hu Jintao, Pretoria, February 2007[2]

The extravagance on show in Beijing at the China Africa Summit that cold November weekend had clearly produced the intended impact. A world looked on in wonder as Chinese and African leaders celebrated their ever-deepening economic and political ties against a backdrop of Chinese acrobatic troupes, African drumming exhibitions, the piercing wail of Peking opera and panoramic tourist posters. And although the international media may have only just discovered the importance of China in Africa at the FOCAC meeting, in many respects the event signalled not the beginning of a relationship but really the end of a decade-long effort of Chinese expansion into the continent that had set the stage for the binding together of the two regions.

Though publicity was a key aim of the summit, in fact it was consolidation of China–Africa relations which became the overriding concern for its hosts. A new three-year action plan was approved by the delegates which would enshrine ties between the two regions within the framework of a 'new strategic partnership'. It included a diplomatic component focused on regular consultation at the UN, the WTO and other multilateral settings; strengthening provincial government exchanges; and working together on areas of common concern such as UN reform and combating terrorism. There was a strong developmental aspect as well, from financial support for expanding African agriculture to the provisions of training programmes in health and the building of educational facilities.[3] The Chinese government committed itself to doubling its ODA, which presumably meant that it would increase from the reported US$44 million in 2005 to US$88 million by 2009. Trade and business, the heart of the new relationship, featured, with US$5 billion worth of concessional loans committed to finance Chinese companies investing in Africa coupled with a pledge to raise two-way trade to US$100 billion by 2010. Finally, reflecting the changing outlook of the Chinese government, even the language of the recent past was updated with the once ubiquitous 'mutual benefit' being subsumed by the business school jargon of forging a 'win-win' relationship, while the overt critiques of Western hegemony of past FOCAC meetings were missing.

Significantly, the problems and discord that had been creeping into the discussions of China's role on the continent were not avoided. The Chinese leadership attempted to tackle these issues head on, recognizing that its firms in Africa were not complying with best standards of business practice on matters of corruption and environmental degradation, and pledging that they would be encouraged to behave in 'an open, fair, just and transparent' way in future.[4] Balanced trade that sought to avoid an unequal exchange mimicking colonial-era ties of commodity exports for finished manufactured goods would be promoted through preferential trade measures such as increasing market access for African exports. This included greater Chinese support for the development of Africa's agriculture sector through technical assistance and direct investment, and extending zero-tariff ratings to 440 products of the less developed African countries. Judicial cooperation to manage criminal activities and illegal migration, problems for both China and African countries, was set in motion.

The attention of the international public had, however, also fallen on China's relations with pariah regimes like Sudan and Zimbabwe. Determined not to shy away from its public policy of non-intervention in African affairs, Chinese authorities were nevertheless increasingly concerned about the damage that these associations could inflict on their international image and rela-tions with the West.[5] Clear signs of Beijing's irritation at the continued unwillingness of Khartoum to abide by international calls to address the situation in Darfur were evident. On the day before the formal opening of FOCAC, the Chinese government released a statement describing how Hu Jintao had urged his Sudanese counterpart, Omar al-Bashir, to demonstrate flexibility in considering UN diplomacy. Even China's willingness to author-ize UN peacekeepers to augment the beleaguered African Union force, subject to Khartoum's approval, represented a shift away from its unconditional defence of the regime in 2004. Despite this change, Chinese policy remained predicated on securing the substantive oil interests it had built up in the country.

The ink was hardly dry on the plenary session's declaration of friendship and the chorus of toasts to hundreds of business deals struck had barely been uttered at the China Africa Sum-mit when the planning for the next stage in relations began. With China's US$1 trillion of foreign reserves being placed in the service of a newly created state investment vehicle, the pos-sibility of dramatic new investments and aid packages was sure to whet African appetites. Coupled with an earlier decision to hold the African Development Bank's annual meeting in Shanghai in May 2007, this looked set to increase China's financial presence on the continent. Another round of diplomatic tours of the African continent commenced on 1 January 2007, led by Foreign Minister Li Zhaoxing, who took in Botswana, the Central African Republic, Guinea-Bissau, Chad and Eritrea. He was followed in February by Hu Jintao, who touched base in Cameroon, Liberia, Sudan, Zambia, Namibia, South Africa, Mozambique and the Seychelles. Once again sidelined by the ferocious pace of Chinese diplomacy towards Africa, the Western media, governments and NGOs could only watch the cavalcade of Chinese political leaders, government officials and businessmen with the now all too familiar sense of concern. An American envoy was belatedly sent to Beijing in the weeks preceding the Chinese president's travels, hoping to gain assurances that China would act decisively in pressuring the Sudanese government.

But in contrast to previous visits to the African continent, though the ubiquitous red carpet and songs of praise that had hitherto accompanied high-profile Chinese diplomacy were still in evidence, the tone of this presidential tour was distinctively different. A new sense of the daunting challenges facing China as it sought to consolidate relations with the continent was apparent, reflecting a new assertiveness from Africa as well as a tangible sense in Beijing of the complexities of managing relations with the continent. Alongside the images of beaming leaders and the standard diplomatic language of shared interests, disquiet and discord greeted the Chinese leader as he announced the now standard array of aid packages, cancellation of debt and new investments in the seven countries visited.

The mood of Africans had clearly begun to change. Liberia's newly elected president, Ellen Johnson-Sirleaf, fresh from having summarily thrown out the unfavourable terms of an iron ore deal with an Indian conglomerate, Mittal, made by her predecessor and renegotiating a better one, was said to be reviewing the terms granted to Chinese investors.[6] In Zambia, the Chinese president had to cancel two symbolically important engagements, a public lecture at the University of Zambia and the launching of a Chinese-sponsored new industrial zone in the Copperbelt, aimed at responding to the anti-Chinese sentiment that featured in the election campaign as well as demonstrating Chinese concern for the mining sector in that country. In both cases these events were cancelled owing to fears that student and trade union protest would disrupt these noteworthy public relations exercises. In Sudan, Africa's pariah regime par excellence, the Chinese soft-power approach came into direct collision with the harsh realities of the Bashir government's dissembling diplomacy and unbridled brutality over the Darfur issue. A putative offer to use Chinese peacekeepers under the UN mandate drew no official response from Khartoum.[7] In the end, the high price of oil dependency on an international 'polecat' was bearable for the Chinese government, but certainly no longer fêted as it once was in Chinese circles.[8] By way of contrast, in Namibia the announcement of a US$250 million concessional loans package marked the onset of serious economic engagement and was met with widespread public approval. And finally in South Africa, the constant news of job losses and firms losing contracts or even closing down owing to Chinese competition had created a constituency of concern around the Chinese presence which spanned the usually fractious ties between the country's trade unions, businessmen and government officials. For South Africans who had become used to a position of continental ascendancy, the multifaceted challenges of China induced specific worries that touched on that country's ambitions and economic standing. Even Mbeki himself felt compelled to publicly state just after the FOCAC summit that the continent should beware of trading traditional Western modes of dominance for a Chinese version.[9]

And at the World Social Forum held in Nairobi that same January 2007, the eclectic gathering of African and other NGOs, anti-globalization activists and development specialists did not trade in diplomatic niceties in their criticism of China's role on the continent. As Humphrey Pole-Pole, head of Tanzania's Social Forum, declared: 'First, Europe and America took over our big businesses. Now China is driving our small and medium entrepreneurs to bankruptcy. You don't even contribute to employment because you bring in your own labour.' The secretary-general of the newly formed China International NGO Network, Cui Janjun, rebutted: 'We Chinese had to make the same hard decision on whether to accept foreign investment many, many years ago. You have to make the right decision or you will lose, lose, lose. You have to decide right, or you will remain poor, poor, poor.'[10] In many ways, celebration of the resurgent China–Africa relations so recently to be heard in Beijing suddenly seemed to sound slightly hollow and more defensive.

Understanding China's role in Africa

The central question here is whether China's role in Africa can best be characterized as that of development partner, economic competitor or colonizer. It should be evident by now that these characterizations oversimplify what are complex and overlapping interactions which are themselves nested within the diverse African political and economic landscape. And, in consequence of the ever-increasing ties, throwing the spotlight on a particular incident or event will at best capture momentarily a feature of the relations that cannot be mistaken for the whole. It is the case, however, that perceptions of relations can be shaped in fundamental ways by these singular examples. For instance, China's close links with the obdurate regime in Khartoum have become a proxy in many eyes, however inaccurate, for its entire engagement with the African continent. In that sense, in many ways its contemporary relations exhibit dimensions of all three characterizations, or at least contribute to the perception inherent in each of the categories of partner, competitor and colonizer.

China is indeed Africa's partner and, in many ways, the continent's most enduring one. From the outset of the establishment of the People's Republic of China to the present day, the Chinese government has pursued a foreign policy that has conformed to the interests and needs of Africans to a greater degree than any other external power. Physical distance and economic standing may have contributed considerably to this, some would argue definitively so, but none the less it remains a historical fact. This is not to say that China's Africa policy wasn't conpatible with its geostrategic concerns, such as Sino-Soviet rivalry or its 'one-China' policy, but rather that even in this context Beijing was able to pursue an approach that reflected shared anti-colonial aims and development aspirations. At the same time, China's role in Africa today is much more profound than in the past and is facing challenges that come with heightened complexity. With the relationship increasingly buttressed by interests and practices that privilege elite ties over the 'new-found' social responsibility discourse promoted by the West, the nature of the partnership will continue to come under scrutiny. Extending that partnership to ensure that the needs of ordinary Africans are met has to be a priority if it is to retain this moniker. The rise of Asian-African business networks in some sectors in some countries, mimicking the 'flying geese' paradigm that was seminal in South-East Asia's development, is a potential harbinger of a positive form of economic cooperation with significant implications for Africa.

In the main China is not a competitor owing to the complementarity of the two regions' economies, one being primarily a supplier of raw materials and the other primarily a producer of manufactured goods. But this general insight masks the larger truth that if Africa wishes to develop its economy and raise its population out of poverty, as did China, it will need to move beyond merely being a resource exporter to the outside world. So in this sense, key aspects of Chinese engagement are clearly competitive with established African businesses, be they South African MNCs, smaller African textile and manufacturing concerns or retail traders. Moreover, before it became a leading exporter of FDI to the continent, China could be said to be a serious competitor for foreign investment in Africa. Finally, in so far as all this competition contributes to the restriction of the development and diversification of African economies, then China will be seen as an economic rival.

Claims that China is planning to colonize Africa are spurious and overblown. In particular, the hallmarks of colonialism – the ideology of a 'civilizing mission', the accompanying territorial imperative and forging of exclusionary trade relations – are distinctly lacking in China's Africa policy. The close proximity between Chinese economic engagement and African elites, however, especially those characterized as 'pariah regimes', will influence attitudes both in Africa and the West to China's underlying aims and ambitions for the continent.[11] In the same way, the rising tide of Chinese migration will continue to raise this spectacle among some Africans (and foreigners) and will therefore, whether Beijing likes it or not, hold implications for China's relations with Africa.

The fact of the matter is that China's engagement in Africa is evolving over time, owing partly to changing strategic rationales and partly to new circumstances encountered by China as its links with the continent extend and deepen. As the relationship moves beyond the declaratory phase of the initial decade of contact, so too will the China–Africa ties become, in a word, 'normalized'. Grand statements of intent are fast being replaced by real-life experiences in the commercial sphere, be they those of the Chinese-owned mining concern in Zambia or the Chinese retailers in the Horn of Africa. In future, China–Africa relations will increasingly be determined not by Beijing or the African elites but rather by the experiences of Africans and Chinese on the ground. The behaviour of thousands of newly settled Chinese businessmen and the conduct of the African communities in which they live and work will matter as much as the diplomacy and concessions made at government level. In this the boundaries of the relationship will be set in ways that will determine the long-term success or failure of Chinese initiatives in Africa.

The future

It is clear that the challenge for any analyst of China's everburgeoning ties with Africa is pinning down a perspective on this fast-moving, omni-dimensional relationship. Despite the pace of change in ties, however, there is enough evidence to make some general observations as to the future of China–Africa relations. Five 'images' of China are set to shape the relationship with Africa: first its image as the new face of globalization; second its role in African development success; third as a mirror for the West; fourth as a pariah partner; and, finally as a responsible stakeholder. These themes provide both important markers of the past and signposts to the future of Chinese–African relations.

China as the new face of globalization For many Africans, the rhetorical debate about its status in the world economy was tied to presumptions of the immutability of Western economic and political dominance over African concerns. One can see this in the oddly quaint anti-Western rhetoric that accompanied the G8 summit in Gleneagles in 2005, the kneejerk response of anti-capitalists to the collusion between Western governments and their leading corporations and their African counterparts.[12] America and the West generally were seen to be the vanguard of globalization and a threat to development aspirations and the daily needs of ordinary Africans, themselves locked in inescapable poverty.

China's rapid ascendancy may have caught the academics and activists off guard but for African workers and business owners alike there is no doubt as to where the competition is coming from. China's phenomenal growth and the ability of its businesses – be they state-affiliated MNCs or family-owned retail shops – to outbid, outsupply and outproduce any African firms (indeed, most Western ones for that matter) make it an apparently unstoppable juggernaut in terms of capturing market share. Tied to this is the productivity of its labour force, which has demonstrated in the African setting its willingness to work long hours in sometimes dire conditions in order to complete the assigned task. For these reasons, increasingly it is China which is supplanting the West as the new face of globalization in Africa and one towards which Africa is formulating responses.

How China manages this fundamental shift in African perceptions is one of the challenges confronting the consolidation of ties with the continent. Deborah Brautigam believes that Chinese development assistance and FDI can provide the right conditions for Africa's 'take-off':

> Chinese factories offer not only jobs – they also use production technologies that African entrepreneurs can easily adopt. The World Bank estimates that African elites keep some 40 percent of their wealth outside the continent, far more than the Asian average of only 6 percent. Chinese firms as catalysts and models could offer incentives for some of that wealth to return to a capital-starved region, much as Japan did when its firms began to relocate to Southeast Asia's 'little tigers' decades ago, and as Korea did in Bangladesh.[13]

China as development model Once again, African elites have discovered and are enamoured of the dramatic and tangible successes of China. In the 1960s, overwhelmed by the glorious portrayal of Chinese agrarian society epitomized by the famous collective farm at Dazhai, African leaders such as Julius Nyerere put Tanzania on a socialist road that unfortunately led to a fall in agricultural productivity and nascent rebellion. Less overtly imitative versions of this model were introduced in Mozambique and Burkina Faso and produced similarly disastrous results. The efficacy of Mao's guerrilla warfare provided its own cadre of African adherents, with Jonas Savimbi, trained at the military academy in Nanjing, being one noted example. Today, while socialist practices have long since been pruned from the Chinese development experience through a lengthy process of trial and error, the impulse to find a 'Chinese model' that can be transferred to the African condition remains strong.

The Chinese's willingness to experiment in defiance of collectivist dogma has been the hallmark of their approach to development. Perhaps where Africans can best apply the Chinese experience of 'reform and opening' is in the application of selectively engaging foreign investors – including China – of all stripes and ensuring that their inputs subscribe to the task of fostering African development. To the credit of the Chinese government, where African governments have presented a concerted complaint or concern, it has usually responded to ameliorate the worst effects in some way. For instance, certain features of the structuring and implementation of Chinese ODA and investment, such as the use of unskilled Chinese labourers, are self-evidently not particularly conducive to reducing African employment needs. Where governments or joint venture companies have insisted on a 'local labour content' clause, the Chinese have proved willing to allow for it or at least introduce 'offsets' such as training programmes.

The last word on adapting the Chinese model to African conditions should be reserved for its key founder, Deng Xiaoping.

When asked to address the suitability of the Chinese experience for Africa during a meeting with Jerry Rawlings, the leader of Ghana, in 1985, Deng said: 'Please don't copy our model. If there is any experience on our part, it is to formulate policies in light of one's own national conditions.'[14]

China as a mirror for the West Another measure of the impact that China's foray into Africa has made can be found in the heightened insecurities displayed by external powers to its sudden irruption into what was once their exclusive sphere of influence. In this respect, the experience of China's global rise and in particular its 'thrust' into Africa holds up a mirror to the West which underscores that its own standing as global leader is under review. Moreover, it casts a rather unflattering reflection on Western conduct in China and, with that, a prevailing sense of Western hypocrisy over the criticism levelled at China's conduct in Africa when its own relations have been barely above reproachable (if not much worse).

In fact, Western criticism of the behaviour of Chinese firms or the proximity of Chinese governments to pariah regimes in many respects smacks of double standards. China exports the capitalism it knows. One must remember that it is a country that has been the second-largest recipient of Western FDI for over two decades. The attraction of setting up or relocating manufacturing to Shenzen or Pudong district for Western investors is precisely the shockingly low wages of Chinese workers and the absence (or lack of enforcement) of labour standards or environmental regulations that impose higher costs on production at home. No serious or sustained concern was expressed by Western corporations, nor was there much fuss made by Western governments, as to these conditions, much less human rights, in China throughout this period. Indeed, the 'no holds barred' approach of many foreigners towards working in China and Chinese society generally certainly set a remarkable standard of blatant arrogance, overt decadence and even at times outright depravity that Chinese entrepreneurs in Africa have yet to visibly aspire to, much less achieve. Again, as the Tiananmen Square massacre faded into the annals of history, the criticisms of human rights voiced by Western governments were drowned out by those interests eager to secure their slice of China's proverbial 'one billion consumers'.

For these reasons, it is not hard to understand why the Chinese view Western protestations – even those by 'right-thinking' Western firms and NGOs – aimed at Chinese businesses in Africa as being more than a little self-serving. Western investment made the China of today in this image (with the active collusion of the Chinese leadership, it must be said), a position that the current government in Beijing is trying to temper through environmental regulation and anti-corruption drives. To suddenly demand a different standard of conduct from Chinese multinational corporations operating in Africa than those subscribed to by Western businesses in China itself seems to hide another agenda.

China as a partner of pariahs The Chinese leadership needs to look carefully at the French experience in Africa. The close relationship between French business and political interests, manifested by the presence of oil company executives in the inner circle in the Elysée Palace, as well as the circulation of key political figures such as Jean-Christophe Mitterrand within political and business circles, has been a feature of France's post-independence Africa policy from the outset.[15] Moreover, the modus operandi of foreign policy-makers in Paris has been to construct policy around a network of personal relationships with individual African leaders, bolstered by a web of bilateral agreements in trade, finance, development assistance and defence.[16] The result has been, much to the dismay of many in France, a convergence between oil company and national armaments industry interests and the government's development policy, such that, in its worst manifestations, French troops have been sent into African countries to quell popular uprisings against local dictators.[17] Much of the thrust of the seemingly perennial efforts to reform France's Africa policy has been aimed, with limited success, at untangling this complex set of relations with the continent. Already Beijing is learning that its ties to Khartoum bring with them any number of unanticipated problems. The spectacle of activists organizing an international boycott of the Beijing Olympics based on Chinese involvement in Sudan underscores this point.

Of equal concern is the rising influence of provincial and municipal authorities over the actual conduct of China–Africa relations. Given that China's renewed engagement with Africa is driven by economic concerns, so sub-state actors are beginning to have a large hand in shaping ties. Provincial and municipal authorities, the enterprises and individuals whom they promote, have a 'chequered' record when it comes to adherence to law and labour and environmental standards. Their wilful pursuit of the narrowest forms of self-interest can do considerable damage to China's standing in Africa. In this way, the contrary goals that have bedevilled Beijing in its approach to managing the 'opening and reform' process between the centre and the provinces seem set to be replicated in the management of its Africa policy. Addressing this troubling dynamic is one of the key challenges for consolidation of China's presence on the continent.

China as responsible stakeholder Much of what China has done in Africa has provided benefit; some things have not. Greater involvement on the continent has already brought about exposure to the vagaries of African politics and, with that, the first movements away from China's rhetorical commitment to non-intervention. This is reflected in the change of tactics over

Sudan, which, as Shi Yinhong has suggested, is linked to its desire to repair the damage done to relations with the West and other African states: '[Hu Jintao] wants to persuade Sudan to not reject the UN resolution and to cooperate with the UN. This will bring moral and diplomatic pressure on Sudan and also help China's ties with the US, the European Union and greater Africa.'[18] There are indications that in the economic sphere there may be changes forthcoming that will bring China closer to Western practices. For instance, Li Ruogu, president of the China Exim Bank, has said that he wants to put his institution on a sounder commercially oriented basis and, in so doing, reduce its reliance on state subsidies.[19] An agreement struck in May 2007 between the China Exim Bank and the World Bank is a further reflection of this trend. Concerned Africans and Westerners should recognize this process and encourage its development in ways that enhance accountability and contribute to African needs. Working together with governments, be they African or Western, and civil society to address the massive structural problems and immediate needs of poverty and conflict has to be a priority for all. In this regard, what China must realize is that not all commentary from African and Western NGOs is either ill founded or even anti-Chinese. NGOs are, to all intents and purposes, the conscience of their respective societies. In the case of the West, they shape the outlook of G8 governments to a degree unknown in other regions, and this unprecedented influence means that Western NGOs' influence over their governments' foreign policy towards Africa is disproportionate to their size. China would be ill advised to ignore them. Concurrently, a sense of humility among Western governments is surely in order: after all, provisions for human rights are at best features of rhetoric in, for example, Uzbekistan and Pakistan, erstwhile American allies in the 'war on terror'. National interest clearly determines Western government positions on these questions, so it should not be a surprise to see this as a guide in some aspects of China's foreign policy as well.

Conclusion

Surveying the ideological period of Chinese relations with Africa in the 1960s and 1970s, Philip Snow observed that: '[A] frank quest for profits by both China and its African partners might well, in the end, prove a more solid basis for their future relationship than the continuing attempt to sustain a rhetorical unity which has sometimes disguised the pursuit of profoundly different goals.'[20] We have now arrived at that point. Although the Chinese government likes to make much of the long history of ties between its society and Africa, the fact of the matter is that it is exactly the opposite conditions – a relatively clean slate of historical experience – which prevail and which have allowed China a free hand in shaping relations with Africa. But now, as the contemporary experience and historical record begin to take shape, the complexities of sustaining these ties will predominate. The Chinese government could rightly claim a status as Africa's key development partner, the most responsive to African concerns and most willing to review and reconsider its approach in light of experience. And though the era of ideological engagement had long since fallen before the exigencies of economic nationalism, the imagery and actions of the past continued to find expression in the management of official relations. This is unlike the situation in the West, where the impulse to 'preach to the fallen heathens' remained so deeply ingrained as to be unrecognized by its own, sometimes well-meaning, progenitors.

Seen from an African perspective, the most significant dimension of Chinese engagement is that it is a potential source of investment capital and development assistance which Western sources are either uninterested in or unwilling to provide. The fact that China joins the bidding for projects enables African governments to broaden the range of potential players and raises the financial stakes in its favour. Indeed, cooperation between Chinese and Indian oil companies is motivated by their mutual concern that they are effectively bidding up the price for such resources. How African governments manage and exploit such international competition is another matter. Sharing a common history of exploitation by imperialists, victimized through externally funded civil wars and subjected to calamitous socialist projects in the name of idealism, the two regions have experiences that can serve as a strong basis for partnership. Whether China's enhanced role in Africa will serve as a catalyst for African development, or whether instead it is shaped by the now familiar mould of an external power pursuing narrow self-interest, remains to be seen. If China is able to adapt itself to African concerns, while pursuing its own broader aims on the continent, then its presence will continue to be well received by Africans. In any case, unlike in the past, it is Africans – not Westerners – who will determine the nature and depth of China's engagement in African affairs.

Notes

Introduction

1 Lu Yu, 'The Merchant's Joy', *Columbia Book of Chinese Poetry*, trans. Burton Watson (New York: Columbia University Press, 1985), p. 321.

1 China's new foreign policy towards Africa

1 Andrea Goldstein and Nicolas Pinaud, 'China's boom: what's in it for Africa?', in Ricardo Soares de Oliveira, Dan Large and Chris Alden (eds), *China Returns to Africa* (London: C. R. Hurst, forthcoming), p. 15.

2 On 'Three Worlds', see William Tow, 'The international strategic system', in Thomas Robinson and David Shambaugh (eds), *Chinese Foreign Policy: Theory and Practice* (Oxford: Clarendon Press, 1994), p. 130; Stephen Levine, 'Perception and ideology in Chinese foreign policy', in ibid., pp. 43–44.

3 Levine, 'Perception and ideology', p. 44.

4 CSIS/IIE, *China: The Balance Sheet* (Washington, DC: Center for Strategic and International Studies/Institute for International Economics, 2006), p. 19.

5 Ibid., p. 18. See also Andy Rothman, *Harmonious Society*, CLSA Report, May 2007.

6 Deng Xiaoping, cited in David Shambaugh (ed.), *Deng Xiaoping:*

Portrait of a Chinese Statesman (Oxford: Clarendon Press, 1995), p. 156.

7 David Zweig and Bi Jianhai, 'The foreign policy of a resource hungry state', *Foreign Affairs*, 84(5), 2005. A top official at the ministry of land and resources, Wang Jia-Shu, characterized the new geopolitics of oil in the aftermath of the US intervention in Iraq in the typically robust language of the strategist: 'China's oil geopolitical imperative in regards to strategy is: focus the attack on neighbouring countries, hold firm in the Middle East, develop Africa.' Wang Jia-Shu, 'China's petroleum security and geopolitics' *Resources and Industries*, 6: 1 2004, cited in Ben Mayo, 'Energy security and chinese foreign policy', unpublished dissertation, London School of Economics, September 2006, p. 17.

For an overview of China–Africa relations in the 1970s and 1980s see Ian Taylor, *China and Africa: Engagement and Compromise* (London: Routledge, 2006). For an account of China–South Africa ties see Garth Le Pere and Garth Shelton, *China, Africa and South Africa: South–South Co-operation in a Global Era* (Midrand: Institute for Global Dialogue, 2007).

8 British Petroleum, *Statistical Review of World Energy*, June 2006.

9 Harry Broadman, *Africa's Silk Road: China and India's New Economic Frontier* (Washington, DC: World Bank, 2006), p. 6.

10 For statistics, see Goldstein and Pinaud, 'China's Boom'.

11 See Raphael Kaplinsky, Dorothy McCormick and Mike Morris, *The Impact of China on Sub-Saharan Africa*, Institute of Development Studies, Sussex University, April 2006; Andrea Goldstein, Nicolas Pinaud, Helmet Reisen and Xiaobao Chen, *The Rise of China and India: What's in It for Africa?* (Paris: OECD Development Centre Studies, 2006).

12 Elling N. Tjonneland et al., 'China in Africa: implications for Norwegian foreign and development policies' (Oslo: Chr. Michelsen Institute, 2006), p. 35; Abah Ofon, 'South–South cooperation: can Africa thrive with Chinese investment?', in Leni Wild and David Mepham (eds), *The New Sinosphere: China in Africa* (London: IPPR, 2006), pp. 26–7.

13 Embassy of China in South Africa, 'China's Africa policy', Pretoria, January 2006.

14 *People's Daily*, 16 December 2003, <www.englishpeopledaily.com.cn>.

15 Cited in Ian Taylor, 'Chinese oil diplomacy in Africa', *International Affairs*, 82(5), 2006, p. 12.

16 For historical accounts of Chinese–Africa relations, see Philip Snow, *The Star Raft* (London: Longman, 1988).

17 Adapted from WTO data, International Trade Statistics 2006 online (1995–2005); and MOFCOM Statistics online (January–November 2006).

18 As described by He Wenping, '"All weather friends": a vivid portrayal of contemporary political relations between China and Africa', in Kinfe Abraham (ed.), *China Comes to Africa: The Political Economy and Diplomatic History of China's Relations with Africa* (Addis Ababa: Ethiopian International Institute for Peace and Development, 2005), p. 41. For another account, see Jonathan Spence, *The Search for Modern China* (London: Norton, 1990), pp. 54–6.

19 'SA's ancient Chinese connection', *Mail and Guardian* (Johannesburg), 7 December 2001.

20 Adapted from WTO data, International Trade Statistics 2006 online.

21 'Oil, global influence driving Hu Jintao's trip', Inter Press Service (Johannesburg), 29 January 2007.

22 Reflected in academic accounts – for example, Garth le Pere and Garth Shelton, 'Afro-Chinese relations: an evolving South–South partnership', *South African Journal of International Affairs*, 13(1), 2006, pp. 33–55.

23 Source: MOFCOM Statistics online (January–November 2006).

24 See examples provided in Chris Alden and Mills Soko, 'South Africa's economic relations with Africa: hegemony and its discontents', *Journal of Modern African Studies*, 43(3), 2005, p. 389.

25 See Ian Taylor, 'Taiwan's foreign policy in Africa: the limits of dollar diplomacy', *Journal of*

Contemporary China, 11(30), 2002. For an overview of Taiwanese diplomacy, see Gary Rawnsley, *Taiwan's Informal Diplomacy and Propaganda* (Basingstoke, 2000); Richard Payne and Cassandra Veney, 'Taiwan and Africa: Taipei's continuing search for international recognition', *Journal of African and Asian Studies*, 36(4), 2001. For the implications and diplomatic interplay between Beijing and Taipei, see Chris R. Hughes, *Chinese Nationalism in a Global Era* (London: Routledge, 2006).

26 These are, as of March 2007, Swaziland, São Tome and Principe, Gabon, Malawi and Burkina Faso.

27 BBC Monitoring Asia, 15 December 2003.

28 Deborah Brautigam, *Chinese Aid and African Development* (New York: St Martin's Press, 1998), pp. 44–6.

29 Ibid., pp. 49–50.

30 Ibid.

31 Information supplied by the South African Treasury to author.

32 Todd Mass and Sarah Rose, 'China Exim Bank and Africa: new lending, new challenges', Center for Global Development, Washington, DC, November 2006, p. 1. The China Development Bank also plays a role, if a less prominent one, in Africa.

33 Ibid., p. 2. Harry Broadman gives a figure of US$12.5 billion. Broadman, *Africa's Silk Road*, pp. 249–50.

34 Mass and Rose, 'China Exim Bank', pp. 2–3. Li Ruogu, president of the China Exim Bank, has suggested that this may change as the bank reduces its reliance on state subsidies. 'China Eximbank reports narrowing losses, falling NPLs', Xinhua News Agency, 22 January 2007.

35 See Ian Taylor, 'China's oil diplomacy in Africa', *International Affairs*, 82(5), 2006.

36 Mark Curtis and Claire Hickson, 'Arming and alarming? Arms exports, peace and security', in Wild and Mepham (eds), *The New Sinosphere*, p. 37; Tjonneland et al., 'China in Africa', p. 13.

37 See Norinco website, <www.norinco.com>. They also manage a small oil company, Zhenghua Oil Company, which is involved in Angola, Gabon and more recently Venezuela.

38 Curtis and Hickson, 'Arming and alarming?', p. 38.

39 As of 2006, Chinese peace-keeping forces in Liberia numbered 566 troops, five police officers and five military observers, in DRC 218 troops and fourteen military advisers and in Sudan 443 troops and fifteen police and fifteen military observers. Cited in Tjonneland et al., 'China in Africa', p. 13.

40 Liu Guijin, Chinese ambassador to South Africa, 'Economic and trade relations between China and Africa', Press release, Pretoria, January 2007.

41 See Taylor, 'China's oil diplomacy in Africa'.

42 Lu Ning, 'The Central Leadership, Supriministry Coordinating Bodies, State Council Ministries and Party Departments', in David Lampton (ed.), *The Making of*

Chinese Foreign and Security Policy in the Era of Reform, 1978–2000 (Stanford, CA: Stanford University Press, 2001), pp. 39–60.

43 For a list of significant Chinese policy-makers and bureaucrats with African expertise, see *Africa Confidential*, 47(14), 7 July 2006, p. 3.

44 For an overview of that process, see Chris Alden, 'Solving South Africa's Chinese puzzle: democratic foreign policy making and the "two Chinas" question', in Jim Broderick et al., *South Africa's Foreign Policy: Dilemmas of a New Democracy* (Basingstoke: Palgrave, 2001).

45 These include Windhoek and Shanghai, Tsumeb and Lanzhou and Mariental and Zhingzhou. Gregor Dobler, 'Solidarity, xenophobia and the regulation of Chinese businesses in Namibia', in Soares de Oliveira et al., *China Returns to Africa*, p. 19.

46 Centre for Chinese Studies, 'China's interest and activity in Africa's construction and infrastructure sectors', Stellenbosch University/ Department for International Development, December 2006 , p. 83.

47 'Chinese province signs MOU in cooperation with Nigerian state', *People's Daily* online, 28 March 2007.

48 'Osun–Chinese govt sets up N5.3 billion pharmaceutical factory', *This Day* (Lagos), 3 December 2006. Peter Cheung and James Tang, 'External relations of China's provinces', in Lampton, *The Making of Chinese Foreign and Security Policy*, p. 115.

49 Carol Lee Hamrin, 'Elite politics and foreign relations', in Robinson and Shambaugh, *Chinese Foreign Policy*, p. 92; Jude Howell, *China Opens Its Doors: The Politics of Economic Transition* (Boulder, CO: Lynne Rienner, 1993), pp. 22–21.

50 Cheung and Tang, 'External relations of China's provinces', p. 100.

51 Ibid., pp. 99–103.

52 Howell, *China Opens Its Doors*, p. 21; Madelyn Ross, 'China's international economic behaviour', in Robinson and Shambaugh, *Chinese Foreign Policy*, p. 448. As Bates Gill and James Reilly note, conflicting bureaucratic responsibilities over SOEs in Africa, with authority divided between the Ministry of Commerce, the provincial governments and the national state-owned Assets Supervision and Administration Commission, coupled to the overarching profit drive, are contributing to problems in host countries in Africa. Bates Gill and James Reilly, 'The tenuous hold of China Inc. in Africa', *Washington Quarterly*, 30(3), summer 2007, p. 45.

53 According to some accounts, Jiang Zemin wrote to the OAU in 1999 to suggest the idea of a China–Africa summit. On US initiatives, see Chris Alden, 'From neglect to virtual engagement: the United States and its new paradigm for Africa', *African Affairs*, 99(396), 2000.

54 See, for example, a discussion of this phenomenon in Ian Phiminster, 'Mugabe, Mbeki and

the politics of anti-imperialism', Afrika Im Kontext Conference, University of Hanover, 2–4 February 2004, p. 5.

55 At the end of apartheid, there were reportedly 485 Taiwan-owned firms which had invested in the Bantustans. John Pickles and Jeff Woods,'Taiwanese investment in South Africa', *African Affairs*, 88(353), 1989, pp. 515–22.

56 This section is drawn from Alden, 'Solving South Africa's Chinese puzzle', pp. 119–38.

57 International Crisis Group, 'Back towards war?', Policy Briefing 111, 1 June 2006.

58 Ato Addis Ainesa, 'Relations between Ethiopia and China: an Ethiopian perspective', in Abraham, *China Comes to Africa*, pp. 242–3.

2 The Chinese in Africa

1 Ben Mayo, 'Energy security and Chinese foreign policy', Unpublished dissertation, LSE, September 2006, p. 12.

2 Howell, *China Opens Its Doors*, pp. 193–4.

3 Ensuk Hong and Laixiang Sun, 'Dynamics of internationalisation and outward investment: Chinese corporations' strategies', *China Quarterly*, 187, 2006, pp. 610, 620.

4 Ibid., p. 611.

5 'China's merchant adventurers set out in search of global conquest', *Financial Times* (London), 16 March 2005. See also Chris Alden and Martyn Davies, 'Chinese business in Africa', *South African Journal of International Affairs*, 13(1), 2006, pp. 83–96.

6 Including the original decision to bring the DRC into the Southern African Development Community.

7 John Daniel and Jessica Lutchman, 'South Africa in Africa: scrambling for energy', in Skhela Buhlungu et al. (eds), *State of the Nation, South Africa 2005–2006* (Cape Town: Human Sciences Research Council, 2006), pp. 499–500.

8 'China: greasing wheels in Africa', *Energy Compass*, 20 January 2006.

9 'CNOOC dives into murky waters in Nigeria', *Petroleum Intelligence Weekly*, 16 January 2006. See also Erica Downs, 'The Chinese energy security debate', *China Quarterly*, 177, March 2004, pp. 21–41.

10 'Big China miner looks abroad', *Dow Jones*, 31 January 2007.

11 'With China calling, is it time to say goodbye to US and Europe?', *The Nation* (Nairobi), 14 April 2006.

12 Cited in the *Oil Daily*, 9 Feburary 2006.

13 Centre for Chinese Studies, 'China's interest and activity in Africa's construction and infrastructure sectors', pp. 21–3.

14 'The increasing importance of Africa's oil', COMTEX, 21 March 2006; 'China's Africa safari', *Fortune* (Asia edition), 20 February 2006.

15 Douglas Yates, 'Chinese oil interests in Africa', Unpublished paper, pp. 5–6.

16 'China's Africa Safari'.

17 See, for example, the SABC news broadcast, 14 April 2006.

18 Centre for Chinese Studies, 'China's interest and activity in

Africa's construction and infrastructure sectors', p. 26.

19 'Alarm bells', *Financial Mail* (Johannesburg), 24 March 2006, pp. 38–9.

20 Centre for Chinese Studies, 'China's interest and activity in Africa's construction and infrastructure sectors', p. 69. Notably, the study found no evidence of the often decried use of 'prison labour' by the Chinese.

21 Ibid., p. 11.

22 CSIS/IIE, *China: The Balance Sheet* (Washington, DC: Center for Strategic and International Studies/Institute for International Economics, 2006), pp. 23–4. The reduction cost 25 million unemployed, this sector having formerly employed 80 per cent of all of Chinese workers.

23 Hong and Sun, 'Dynamics of internationalisation and outward investment', p. 624.

24 Ibid., p. 625.

25 Deborah Brautigam, 'Close encounters: Chinese business networks as industrial catalysts in sub-Saharan Africa', *African Affairs*, 102, 2003.

26 Gillian Hart, 'Global connections: the rise and fall of a Taiwanese production network on the South African periphery', Institute of International Studies, Working Paper 6, University of California, Berkeley, 1996; Janet Wilhelm, 'The Chinese communities in South Africa', in Buhlungu et al. (eds), *State of the Nation*, p. 358.

27 Deborah Brautigam, 'Flying geese or hidden dragon? Chinese business and African development',

Paper presented at the Conference on China–Africa Relations, Cambridge University, 12–13 July 2006, pp. 20–22.

28 Cited in ibid., p. 21.

29 Dulue Mbachu, 'Nigerian resources: changing the playing field', *South African Journal of International Affairs*, 13(1), 2006, p. 80.

30 International Labour Organization, 'Africa fears "tsunami" of cheap imports', 18 December 2005, <www.int.iol.co.za>.

31 Mbachu, 'Nigerian resources', p. 80.

32 On Namibia, see Gregor Dobler, 'South–South trade relations: the example of Oshikango, Namibia', Unpublished paper, May 2005. On Cape Verde, see Heidi Ostbo Haugen and Jorgen Carling, 'On the edge of the Chinese diaspora: the surge of *baihuo* business in an African city', *Ethnic and Racial Studies*, 28(4), July 2005, pp. 639–62. On Botswana, see *Mmegi/The Reporter* (Gaberone), 'Mixed reaction to Chinese invasion', 24 May 2005. On Angola, author interviews in Huambo, September 2005.

33 Cited in 'China treads on Western toes in Africa', *Financial Times Deutschland*, 19 January 2007.

34 Gregor Dobler, 'Solidarity, xenophobia and the regulation of Chinese businesses in Namibia', in Soares de Oliveira et al., *China Returns to Africa*, p. 7.

35 I am basing most of my comments on Haugen and Carling, 'On the edge of the Chinese diaspora', and Dobler, 'Solidarity'.

36 See Melanie Yap and Diane

Man, *Colour, Confusion and Concessions: The History of the Chinese in South Africa* (Hong Kong: Hong Kong UP, 1996).

37 John Pickle and James Woods, 'Taiwanese investment in South Africa', *African Affairs*, 88(353), 1989, pp. 515–22.

38 Frank Pieke, 'Community and identity in the new Chinese migration order', Centre on Migration, Policy and Society, Working Paper no. 24, University of Oxford, 2005, p. 9.

39 Janet Wilhelm, 'The Chinese communities in South Africa', in Buhlungu et al., *State of the Nation*, p. 351.

40 Interview with South African Department of Foreign Affairs officials, 1998; Wilhelm, 'The Chinese communities in South Africa', p. 352. South African government estimates are lower but AsiaNews. it reports a figure of 400,000. 'Hu begins difficult trip to Africa tomorrow', 27 January 2007.

41 Barry Sautman, confirmed by email.

42 Ibid. For a more comprehensive review of Chinese settlement in Africa see Barry Sautman and Yan Hairong, 'Friends and interests: China's distinctive links with Africa', *African Studies Review*, 50(2), September 2007.

43 Barry Sautman, confirmed by email.

44 '40,000 Chinese in Namibia says MP, scramble for Africa on again', *The Namibian*, 21 November 2006. This figure is disputed by Gregor Dobler. See also comments

in P. J. Botha, 'China Inc: an assessment of the implications for Africa – new diplomatic initiatives', in Greg Mills and Natasha Skidmore (eds), *Towards China Inc? Assessing the Implications for Africa* (Braamfontein: South African Institute for International Affairs, 2004), p. 63.

45 According to Guy Scott, Secretary General of the Patriotic Front, as reported in IRIN, 'Cold reception for China's president', 5 February 2007.

46 As reported by the Chinese embassy in DRC to *China Daily*, 26 November 2004, cited at <www.sinoptic.ch/embassy/presses chau/2006/20061120–1124.htm>.

47 Centre for Chinese Studies, 'China's interest and activity in Africa's construction and infrastructure sectors', p. 19.

48 'Confusing Zhing with Zhong', *Financial Gazette* (Harare), 1 February 2007.

49 The only comparative commentary on the number of expatriate whites settled in Africa that I have seen says that there are just 100,000 – a figure which seems too low. Barry Sautman and Yan Hairong, 'Honour and shame? China's Africa ties in comparative context', in Wild and Mepham, *The New Sinosphere*, p. 59.

50 Dobler, 'Solidarity', p. 5.

51 Bates Gill, Chin-hao Huang and J. Stephen Morrison, *China's Expanding Role in Africa: Implications for the United States*, CSIS Report (Washington, DC: Center for Strategic and International Studies, 2007), p. 41. The Chinese govern-

ment did rehouse people affected by the Three Gorges Dam but for many this proved to be inadequate or unappealing.

52 Ibid., pp. 32, 46.

53 Pieke, 'Community and Identity', p. 14.

54 Chen Yi Ding, 'A research on economic globalization and its influences to overseas Chinese economy [*sic*]', *World Regional Studies*, 12(3), September 2003, pp. 14–19. Chen claims that overseas Chinese can serve as a 'bridge' between China, South-East Asia and Africa, ultimately gaining sufficient influence in African politics to further promote economic interests.

55 In Sierra Leone, individual entrepreneurs are said to be primarily from Hunan province. Goldstein et al., *The Rise of China and India*, p. 57.

56 Pieke, 'Community and identity', p. 11.

57 Chinese ambassador to South Africa, Address to African diplomatic corps, Pretoria, 19 January 2006; Ling Guiru, 'China's trade stance with South Africa', *Traders* (Johannesburg), 24, November–February 2006, p. 49.

58 *Business Day* (Johannesburg), 19 April 2006, p. 2.

59 See, for example, the websites for Sinopec and PetroChina.

60 See CNOOC, 'Social responsibility report 2005', pp. 1–39.

61 Yates, 'Chinese oil interests in Africa', p. 15.

62 Cited in *Oil Daily*, 9 February 2006.

63 Ben Schiller, 'The Chinese model of development', Open Democracy, <www.opendemocracy.net>, p. 2.

64 Ibid., p. 2.

3 Africa turns east

1 Dan Large, 'As the beginning ends: China's return to Africa', Pambazuka News, 14 December 2006, <www.pambazuka.org>.

2 For a detailed account see Dan Large, 'Petro politics on the Nile: China's modern relations with Sudan', in Soares de Oliveira et al., *China Returns to Africa*; also Yitzak Schichor, 'Sudan: China's outpost in Africa', China Brief, Jamestown Foundation, 4 November 2005.

3 Sudan Disinvestment UK, 'Matching words with action: how to pressure Sudan to stop its genocidal campaign in Darfur', *Waging Peace*, nd, p. 12.

4 A delegation of the Government of Southern Sudan, led by President Salva Kiir, visited Beijing in March 2005. Xinhau, 'Chinese president meets Sudan's vice presidents', 2 February 2007.

5 Human Rights Watch, 'Report: Sudan and oil', <www.hrw./org/reports/2003/sudan1103/21.htm>.

6 'China–Sudan relations', *Issue Brief*, Small Arms Survey, London, 2007, p. 5. Notably, according to SIPRI, the bulk of Sudan's military equipment is sourced from Russia while France, Iran and Saudi Arabia are suppliers.

7 'Chinese investment sparks economic boom in Sudan', transcript, Public Broadcast Service, *News Hour*, 15 May 2006.

8 This was announced by Mugabe in April 2005 at the Independence Day 'celebrations'. *South Scan*, 20(8), 22 April 2005.

9 Cited in 'Chinese technology for Mugabe's spies', 11 March 2006, <NewZimbabwean.com>.

10 'Zimbabwe: Look East policy failing', Institute for War and Peace Reporting, Africa Report no. 42, 27 September 2005.

11 'Mugabe hails China as Beijing promises Africa aid', Reuters, 15 December 2003.

12 'China snubs country', *Financial Gazette*, 1 February 2007.

13 The loan is payable at 1.7 per cent over seventeen years.

14 *African Confidential*, 41(14), 7 June 2006; Centre for Chinese Studies, 'China's interest and activity in Africa's construction and infrastructure sectors', pp. 23–4.

15 Alex Vines, 'China in Africa: a mixed blessing?' *Current History*, May 2007, pp. 216–18.

16 'China, Nigeria to promote trade', *China Daily*, 27 April 2006.

17 Cited in Sharath Srinivasan, 'Nigeria–China relations: expansion and negotiation as the rising great power embraces Africa', Paper presented at a conference at Cambridge University, July 2006, p. 1.

18 'Local investors condemn incentives to Asians', *This Day* (Lagos), 4 July 2006.

19 'Guangzhou crackdown nets African drug mules', *South China Morning Post*, 12 September 2006; 'Out of Guangzhou, Africa trade booms', *China Daily*, 23 May 2006.

20 Sanusha Naidu, 'South Africa's relations with the People's Republic of China: mutual opportunities or hidden threats?', in Buhlungu et al., *State of the Nation*, p. 457.

21 Ibid.

22 According to other mining companies active in Zambia, the Chinese investors had privileged access to the presidency.

23 'New form of Chinese aid revives Zambia's largest textile factory', *People's Daily,* 27 November 2003.

24 Other reports suggested he shot four miners and the police shot one miner.

25 Yaroslav Trofimov, 'New management: in Africa, China's expansion begins to stir resentment', *Wall Street Journal*, 2 February 2007; also <yaroslv.trofimov.@wsj.com>.

26 See various reports and editorials in the African press.

27 Trofimov, 'New management'.

28 'Kabwe textile firm survival plan coming', *The Times of Zambia*, 30 January 2007.

29 *The Times* (London), 2 February 2007.

30 For one plea for better African coordination see Chris Alden, 'Leveraging the Chinese dragon: towards an Africa that can say no', *E-Africa, Electronic Journal of Governance and Innovation*, February 2005, pp. 6–9 (also published by *Yale Global* – <yaleglobal.yale.edu/display.article?id=5335)>.

31 Various conversations with South African government officials.

32 'Govt, China sign deals

to tune of N$60 million', *The Namibian*, 6 February 2007.

33 'Istanbul Declaration', Global Alliance for Fair Textile Trade, <www.fairtextiletrade.org>.

34 FOCAC pre-meeting, SAIIA-NEPAD-RAS, September 2006, Johannesburg.

35 Personnel claimed that they were restricted from criticizing China after the donation had been made. Off-the-record conversations.

36 Mandisi Mphalwa, Minister for Trade and Industry, South Africa, speaking at the World Economic Forum, Cape Town, 31 May–2 June 2006.

37 Raphael Kaplinsky, 'Winners and losers: China's trade threats and opportunities for Africa', in Wild and Mepham, *The New Sinosphere*, p. 19.

38 Goldstein et al., *The Rise of China and India*, p. 83.

39 International Labour Organization, 'Africa fears "tsunami" of cheap imports'.

40 Source: National Bureau of Statistics of China, *China Statistical Yearbook 2006*, China Statistics Press.

41 Dulue Mbachu, 'Nigerian resources: changing the playing field', *South African Journal of International Affairs*, 13(1), 2006, p. 80; the figure of 350,000 is used in Raphael Kaplinsky, Dorothy McCormick and Mike Morris, *The Impact of China on Sub-Saharan Africa*, Institute of Development Studies, Sussex University, April 2006, p. 8.

42 Andrea Goldstein and Nicolas Pinaud, 'China's boom: what's in it for Africa?', in Soares de Oliveira et al., *China Returns to Africa*, p. 18.

43 'China, W Africa to enhance cotton textile cooperation', *Xinhua*, 6 November 2006.

44 Chinese International Labour Cooperation, *Annual Report*, 2006.

45 Maneul Enes Ferreira, Presentation at China Scramble Conference, Cambridge University, July 2006. The figure of 3 million was derived from the statement of an Angolan minister at a conference on energy issues held in Cape Town in 2005 but, though widely repeated, has never been confirmed.

46 'Zambians attack Chinese businesses', *The Times*, 3 October 2006. *The Times* reported the Chinese community to be 30,000, a figure which is touted by Guy Scott, secretary general of the opposition Patriotic Front, as reported in IRIN, 'Cold reception for China's President', 5 February 2007.

47 Dan Large, Christian Aid report, London, 2007, p. 8.

48 Report supplied by the South African Treasury.

49 Human Rights Watch, 'Report: Sudan and oil', <www.hrw./org/reports/2003/sudan1103/21.htm>.

50 As reported in Ali Abdalla Ali, 'The political economy of the relation between Sudan and China: a brief survey', Paper presented in Pretoria, October 2005, p. 47.

51 'Chinese investment sparks economic boom in Sudan', trans-

cript, Public Broadcast Service, *News Hour*, 15 May 2006.

52 'Thanks China, now go home', *Guardian*, 5 February 2007.

53 Cited in *Mining and Engineering News* (Johannesburg), 9 June 2006.

54 Mohammed Kadala, cited in 'Africa's thriving trade with China', BBC report, *Africa Live!*, nd.

55 Centre for Chinese Studies, 'China's interest and activity in Africa's construction and infrastructure sectors'.

56 'Thanks China, now go home'.

57 'NSHR slams China over its human rights record', *The Namibian*, 5 February 2007.

58 Mandy Mwaseba, *The Post* (Lusaka), 13 September 2006.

59 Henry Lu, museum curator based in Hong Kong, as cited in *China Daily*, 12 July 2004.

60 According to the Nigerian consul-general, Hong Kong, September 2006.

61 According to a West African doctoral student based in Beijing for a number of years.

62 Cited in Jagdish Hiremath, 'Indian foreign policy in Africa: current status and the future', in N. Vohra and K. Mathews (eds), *Africa, India and South–South Co-operation* (New Delhi: Har-Anand, 1997).

63 See Peter Draper and Garth le Pere, *Enter the Dragon: Towards a Free Trade Agreement Between China and the Southern African Customs Union* (Midrand: Institute for Global Dialogue, 2005).

64 IRIN, 'Cold reception for China's president'.

65 Kerstin Canby, 'China and the global market for forest products: look at Russia and Africa', Presentation, Forest Trends, Beijing, July 2006, <www. illegal-logging.info/ papers/presentations/25–260107/ canby1.ppt>.

66 Catherine Mackenzie, 'Forest governance in Zambezia Province: Chinese takeaway!', Report for FOGZA, Maputo, Mozambique, April 2006, <www.illegal-logging.info/ papers/Mozambique_China.pdf>.

67 Ali Askouri, 'China's investment in Sudan: displacing villages and destroying communities', in Firoze Manji and Stephen Marks (eds), *African Perspectives on China in Africa* (Naibori: Fahamu, 2007), pp. 78–81. Three European companies participated in the project as well and have not faced as much public fallout as the Chinese have.

68 Michelle Chan-Fishel, 'Environmental impact: more of the same?', in Manji and Marks, *African Perspectives*, p. 149.

69 Peter Gastrow, 'Triad societies and Chinese organised crime in South Africa', Occasional Paper 48, Pretoria, Institute for Security Studies, 2001.

70 Ibid.

71 'NSHR slams China over its human rights record'.

72 Ndubisi Obiorah, 'Who's afraid of China in Africa? Towards an African civil society perspective on China–Africa relations', in Manji and Marks, *African Perspectives*, pp. 47–9.

73 Diane Games, 'China: the new economic imperialists in Africa', *Business Day* (Johannesburg), 21 February 2005; AfroDad and others at World Social Summit, Nairobi, January 2007.

74 See Chinese mining spokesman's statement cited in Trofimov, 'New management'.

75 'MPs divided over Chinese loan', *Mmegi/The Reporter* (Gaberone), 14 July 2006.

76 Debate over Chinese migration, the impact of Chinese firms and their practices as well as ties to government projects have been discussed in parliaments by opposition parties in Namibia, Botswana and Zimbabwe.

4 Between hope and fear

1 Africa's share of FDI flows was only 1.8 per cent. Broadman, *Africa's Silk Road*, p. 7.

2 In April 2007, the Africa Progress Panel chastised Western donors for the persistent shortfalls in provisions for foreign assistance which would make the Gleneagles commitments impossible to achieve. 'In 2005, G8 pledged US$50 bn for Africa. Now the reality', *Guardian*, 25 April 2007.

3 'China in Africa', *New York Times*, 8 August 2004.

4 'China's Africa safari', *Fortune* (Asia edition), 20 February 2006.

5 This covert operation supplied the MPLA government with vital weapons and related materials in the early 1990s when Unita appeared to be poised to win a military victory. This came at a time

when, by international agreement, there was an embargo on arms sales. See Human Rights Watch, 'The oil diagnostic in Angola: an update', March 2001.

6 'China's Africa safari'.

7 Jeffrey Sachs, cited in 'China makes Africa its business', *New York Times*, 18 August 2006.

8 Chinese assistant foreign minister, cited by the BBC, 27 January 2007.

9 'US–Africa trade profile', US Department of Commerce, <www.agoa.gov>.

10 Tjonneland et al., 'China in Africa', p. 46.

11 See Joshua Cooper Ramo, *The Beijing Consensus* (London: Foreign Policy Centre, 2004).

12 Robert Kagan, 'League of dictators? Why China and Russia will continue to support autocracies', *Washington Post*, 30 April 2006, <www.washingtonpost.com>.

13 Christopher Smith, Deputy Assistant Secretary of State for African Affairs, cited in 'China no threat to United States in Africa, US official says', 28 July 2005, <us.info.state.gov>.

14 See, for example, Department of Defense, 'The military power of the People's Republic of China 2005', Annual Report to Congress, Washington, DC, 2005.

15 Peter Brookes and Ji Hye Shin, 'China's influence in Africa: implications for the United States', Backgrounder Report no. 1916, Heritage Foundation, Washington, DC, 22 February 2006.

16 Council on Foreign Relations, *More than Humanitarianism: A Strategic US Approach Toward Africa* (New York: Council on Foreign Relations, 2005).

17 Gill et al., *China's Expanding Role in Africa*, p. 16.

18 Cited in ibid., p. 15.

19 Marred, unfortunately, by the 7/7 bombings in London during the actual summit.

20 Foreign Minister Jack Straw, Foreign and Commonwealth Office, 14 February 2006.

21 David Fish, DfID, Presentation at the Institute for Public Policy Research conference on China and Africa, London, July 2005.

22 Cited in 'China's "peaceful rise" running into criticism', BBC News, 2 February 2007, <ww.bbc.co.uk>.

23 Cameroon, of course, poses a problem in terms of this spheres-of-influence rubric with its German colonial past overlaid by British and French influence.

24 See Roland Marchal, 'French perspectives on the new Sino-African Relations', in Soares de Oliveira et al., *China Returns to Africa*.

25 In 2003, Paris ignored strenuous protests from the Nordic states, Holland and Great Britain when it invited Robert Mugabe and his entourage to the Franco-African Summit.

26 Crucial for the Chinese National Machinery and Equipment Import and Export Corporation in securing the contract for the iron ore at Belinga was a commitment by the Chinese government to fund road and rail projects linking the remote area to the coast. *Business Day* (Johannesburg), 5 February 2007.

27 See 'China and South Africa: a bilateral relationship or multilateral strategy?', Jetro, Johannesburg, 14 June 2000.

28 For an overview, see Jun Morikawa, *Japan and Africa: Big Business and Diplomacy* (Johannesburg: University of Witwatersrand Press, 1997); Kweku Ampiah, *The Dynamics of Japan's Relations with Africa: South Africa, Tanzania and Nigeria* (London: Routledge, 1997); Chris Alden and Makoto Sato, 'La diplomatie japonaise de l'aide et l'Afrique', *Afrique Contemporaine*, 212, Winter 2004, pp. 13–32; Deborah Sharp, 'Japan and southern Africa: the resource rationale', in Chris Alden and Katsumi Hirano, *Japan and South Africa in a Globalising World: A Distant Mirror* (Aldershot: Ashgate, 2003), pp. 102–20.

29 Ben Schiller, 'The Chinese model of development', Open Democracy, <www.opendemocracy.net>, p. 1.

30 'China trade on Western toes in Africa', *Financial Times* (London), 12 January 2007.

31 This was evident at the conference on China and Africa, London, July 2005.

32 Goldstein and Pinaud, 'China's boom'.

33 Broadman, *Africa's Silk Road*; Raphael Kaplinsky, 'Winners and losers: China's trade threats and opportunities for Africa', in Manji and Marks, *African Perspectives*.

34 According to one seasoned

analyst, African governments' preference for Chinese credit has 'prompted the IMF to switch to unfunded monitoring programs and the World Bank to focus less on measures for improving governance and tackling corruption and more on Africa's adverse business operating environment'. Alex Vines, 'China in Africa', p. 218.

35 'China trade on Western toes in Africa'.

36 Gill et al., *China's Expanding Role in Africa*, p. 19.

37 Joshua Eisenman and Joshua Rogin, 'China must play by the rules in oil-rich Sudan', *Alexander's Gas and Oil Connections*, 8(6), 21 August 2003, p. 1; *Drill Bits and Tailings*, 6(2), 28 February 2001.

38 Interviews with leading investment firms in the City of London, 23 January 2007.

39 Tjonneland et al., 'China in Africa', p. 16.

40 Margaret Pearson, 'The major multilateral economic institutions engage China', in Alastair Johnson and Robert Ross (eds), *Engaging China: The Management of an Emerging Power* (London: Routledge, 1999), pp. 218–22.

41 Zhu Ronji, '5 year plan', *People's Daily*, 5 March 2001.

42 Evan Medeiros, 'China debates its "peaceful rise" strategy', YaleGlobal Online, 22 June 2004, <www.yale.yaleglobal.edu>.

43 Pang Zhongying, 'China's changing attitude to UN peacekeeping', *International Peacekeeping*, 12(1), 2005 ; Mark Curtis and Claire Hickson, 'Arming and alarming?

Arms exports, peace and security', in Wild and Mephma, *The New Sinosphere*, p. 41.

44 Pearson, 'The major multilateral economic institutions engage China', p. 223. She cautions, however, as to the continuing possibilities of this trend of 'norms diffusion' as political centralization loosens its grip.

45 *International Herald Tribune*, 15 August 2005.

46 Gill et al., *China's Expanding Role in Africa*, pp. 159–60.

47 Source: WTO data, International Trade Statistics 2006 online.

48 One Chinese analyst observed that China was in danger of being regarded as a 'reckless country'. See Zha Dojun, cited in Dan Large, 'Petro politics on the Nile: China's modern relations with Sudan', in Soares de Oliveira et al., *China Returns to Africa*, pp. 8, 9.

49 China's special envoy to the region, Liu Guijin, appointed in 2007, went on to describe Khartoum as a naughty child, 'If you judge him to be a bad child, when he does something good you should give him a little encouragement and say some nice things.' Voice of America, 'China takes credit for Sudan allowing UN peacekeepers', 5 July 2007.

50 'China filling void left by West in UN peacekeeping', *Washington Post*, 24 November 2006.

5 Consolidating China–Africa relations

1 'Africa must prevent "colonial" China links – Mbeki', SABC

News, 13 December 2006, <www.sabcnews.com>.

2 Hu Jintao, Address at the University of Pretoria, 7 February 2007.

3 African Renewal, 'Big leap in China ties', United Nations, New York, 19 January 2007.

4 Ibid.

5 Discussions with Chinese officials and academics, various locations/dates.

6 'Liberia: Ellen speaks highly of Mittal steel contract', *The Inquirer* (Monrovia), 9 February 2007.

7 As reported in *Kommersant*, 13 February 2007, <www.kommersant.com>.

8 Angola, China's leading oil source in Africa, dealt its Chinese partners a shock in March 2007 when it reversed the decision to award Sinopec the right to construct the oil refinery in Lobito. Angolan officials cited their concerns that the facility was only aimed at supplying the Chinese market and an unwillingness to be locked into long term supply contracts.

9 'Africa must prevent "colonial" China links – Mbeki'.

10 Walden Bello, 'Beijing's turbo-charged diplomacy sparks debate', *Fahama*, 8 February 2007.

11 An example of this is Ali Askouri, a Sudanese environmental activist, who characterizes China as engaging in 'soft colonization'. See Ali Askouri, 'China investment de-stroying African communities: the case of the Merowe Dam, Sudan' presentation to Wilson Center, Washington, DC, 22 March 2007, <www.wilsoncenter.org>.

12 See Patrick Bond, *Looting Africa: The Economics of Exploitation* (London: Zed Books, 2006).

13 Deborah Brautigam, Online debate, Council on Foreign Relations, 13 February 2007.

14 Cited in Wei Wei Zhang, 'The allure of the Chinese model', *International Herald Tribune*, 1 November 2006, <www.iht.com>.

15 'Five year sentence for former Elf chief', *Guardian*, 12 November 2003.

16 See, for example, John Chipman, *French Power in Africa* (Oxford: Blackwell, 1989).

17 The election of the Socialist Party in 1981 was fought to an extent around Valérie Giscard d'Estaing's close ties with a brutal dictator, the self-styled 'Emperor' Bokassa in the Central African Republic.

18 'Hu's Africa trip fuels controversy', *Al-Jazeera*, 29 January 2007, <Aljazeera.net>.

19 'China Eximbank reports narrowing losses, falling NPLs', Xinhua News Agency, 22 January 2007.

20 Philip Snow, 'China and Africa: consensus and camouflage', in Robinson and Shambaugh, *Chinese Foreign Policy*, p. 321.

Index